PRAISE FOR "NEW INDIAN HOME COOKING"

"A weight-loss cookbook with a very new and welcome flavor . . . provides a sensible guide to preparing delicious, yet nutritious meals, with guidelines on how to improve your health and lifestyle . . . all the ingredients for healthy and tasty meals await your taste buds."

—Independent Publishers

"With traditional Indian dishes from various regions of India, Madhu Gadia presents healthful Indian recipes aplenty. I recommend this book to all those who are looking for healthy Indian recipes. It will be a welcome addition to any kitchen."

—India Currents

"An authentic, albeit low-fat perspective . . . Gadia conveys both a love of her cultural heritage and down-to-earth, easily understood guidelines for healthy eating. A sound resource on Indian cooking from a dietary standpoint."

—ALA Booklist

"Provides even the most novice cook simple recipes that turn out better than the gourmet Indian restaurants I've been to in the United States, Hong Kong and England. A must cookbook for all households that enjoy international cuisine."

—John C. Wacker, Professor, Iowa State University

"Delicious Indian food . . . A to Z. Finally a cookbook everyone can use—from a beginner to an advanced cook, with a nutrition guide for healthful gourmets."

—Francie White, Dietician, Santa Barbara

"Excellent . . . includes good-tasting, slimmed-down versions of everything from palak paneer to tandoori chicken to shrimp in yogurt sauce."

—Tufts University Health and Nutrition Letter

NEW INDIAN
HOME COOKING

MORE THAN 100 DELICIOUS,
NUTRITIONAL, AND EASY
LOW-FAT RECIPES!

Madhu Gadia, M.S., R.D.

HPBooks

HPBooks
Published by The Berkley Publishing Group
A division of Penguin Putnam Inc.
375 Hudson Street
New York, New York 10014

Author photograph by Jacquelyn W. Olson of Jacquelyn's
Cover photograph © by Studio Bonisolli/StockFood Munich
Book design by Richard Oriolo
Cover design by Jill Boltin

Modified Exchange Lists on pages [231–238] used with permission of the
American Dietetic Association.

First edition: August 2000

Published simultaneously in Canada.

The Penguin Putnam Inc. World Wide Web site address is
http://www.penguinputnam.com

LIBRARY OF CONGRESS CATALOGING-IN-PUBLICATION DATA
Gadia, Madhu.
   New Indian home cooking / Madhu Gadia.—1st ed.
      p. cm.
   Includes index.
   ISBN 1-55788-343-2
      1. Cookery, Indic. I. Title.

TX724.5.I4 G35 2000
641.5954—dc21

                                                                    00-027774
PRINTED IN THE UNITED STATES OF AMERICA
10

The recipes contained in this book are to be followed exactly as written.
Neither the publisher nor the author is responsible for your specific health
or allergy needs that may require medical supervision, or for any adverse
reactions to the recipes contained in this book.

TO MOM AND DAD

CONTENTS

PREFACE

Food has a language of its own. "What's for dinner?" is probably the most common question spoken in every language of the world. Something about the aroma of cooking is very soothing to the body and soul. Nothing brings a family together like a home-cooked meal. As a child growing up in India, I remember becoming hungry when the smell of food filled the air. The family would sit down to a meal together and exchange the day's events. Suddenly I felt nourished with both food and love. Another food memory is related to going on the train to my grandmother's house. At the train station I always looked for the same vendor who was famous for his *samosas* (potato-stuffed pastry). His *samosas* were like no one else's we ever ate. These memories are very personal and very close to my heart. A taste or smell of food can take me down memory lane without ever leaving my house.

When I came to America, I wondered if I would be able to get my favorite and familiar foods. My fears were ill-founded. I easily found most of the needed ingredients. If something was not available locally, I could mail order it from Indian grocery stores in large cities. Over the years, the availability of Indian spices and other special ingredients has increased tremendously as more local grocery stores and specialty stores cater to different ethnic populations.

Indian cuisine is becoming increasingly popular in America. Five years ago, I learned that some people in my small city of Ames, Iowa, were interested in learning Indian cooking. I decided to offer a class. As I started to prepare for the class, I realized that I did not have any written recipes. I learned to cook from my mother and she from her mother. The art of cooking in India is passed on in this way from generation to generation. If you asked an Indian friend how to prepare something, he or she would simply tell you, giving approximate measures. Well that would not work in a class setting. So I started writing my own recipes.

A NUTRITIONAL LOOK AT INDIAN FOOD

As a registered dietitian I am always concerned about the nutrient content of foods. Indian meals, with plenty of vegetables, beans and lentils, are generally high in carbohydrates and fiber. The fat content of some Indian dishes may be high, but over the years I have successfully reduced the amount of fat used in preparing many traditional Indian dishes. Reducing the fat content can mean using less fat or it may require variation in spices or cooking techniques. I have experimented and developed the recipes to reduce the fat content while maintaining the traditional flavor and taste.

Vegetarian meals are becoming more acceptable and popular in the Western world. As part of a diet low in saturated fat and cholesterol, reduction in the intake of meat, poultry and fish is recommended. Vegetarian meals are part of the daily diet in India. A significant percentage of Indians are lacto-vegetarians, vegetarians who include dairy products in their diets. Even nonvegetarians in India do not eat meat at every meal or every day, and all auspicious occasions exclude meat because of religious beliefs. Indians have combined beans, vegetables, grains and yogurt in a meal for centuries. The combination of these foods was later classified as a way of getting "complete" protein. Indian vegetarian meals are delicious, exciting and nutritious.

The recipes offered in this book have been carefully tested for accuracy. Several of the recipes were offered in the cooking class and retested by the students. My family, friends and students have enjoyed serving as the official taste testers.

The purpose of this book is to provide recipes for healthy, low-fat, quick, authentic Indian meals that are both delicious and nutritious. For those looking for a little spice in their life, whether following a low-cholesterol diet, a diabetic meal plan or a vegetarian diet; cutting down on fat intake; or simply wanting great-tasting Indian food, this book offers a variety of dishes to please the taste buds.

ACKNOWLEDGMENTS

 I would to take this opportunity to thank the people who helped make this book possible:

My mother, Satya Vati Gupta, for teaching me the art and love of cooking.

My father, Vimal Kishore Gupta, for his world of wisdom and love of life.

My husband, Shashi, for his love, support and encouragement.

My daughter, Manisha, and son, Nitin; they were always eager to try the recipes. They give me strength and make cooking fun for me.

My editor, Jeanette Egan, for taking the time to understand a new culture and its idiosyncrasies. She made it easy for me to write and sometimes even helped me clarify my own thinking.

My agent, Bob Silverstein, for bringing this book to light. He saw the potential in the original book, *Lite and Luscious Cuisine of India*, and knew the right contacts.

My brother, Ajay Gupta; he has always been there for me. My sisters, Veena, Meenakshi and Shelly, for their encouragement, love and support. I can call any of them and get recharged. Without their support it would be a lonely road.

My friends, Vandana Kothari, Amita Dayal, Rema Nilakanta, Sunanda Vittal, Simi Giri, Rama Sridhar, Jayati Mitra, Krishna Athreya, Rajashree Agarwal, Aruna Vedula for their friendship and support. They have shared numerous recipes and personal family stories as our families shared meals together. Through them I have traveled India in my dining room.

My aunti and friend, Sadhna Agarwal, for her enthusiasm and support.

My mausi (aunt) Urmil Bansal for her love and excitement.

Thanks to all the people who took my cooking classes. Their enthusiasm to learn new cuisine and taste for Indian food gave me a head start.

My clients, who come to decipher nutrition information and take better care of their bodies. They make my job fun and exciting. I learn so much from them.

INDIA

Jammu and Kashmir

Himachal Pradesh

Punjab

Haryana

Delhi

Rajasthan

Uttar Pradesh

Bihar

Sikkim

Assam

Arunachal Pradesh

Nagaland

Manipur

Mizoram

Tripura

Meghalaya

West Bengal

Gujarat

Madhya Pradesh

Orissa

Maharashtra

Andhra Pradesh

Goa

Karnataka

Kerala

Tamil Nadu

THE CUISINE OF INDIA

FROM KASHMIR IN THE NORTH TO KANYAKUMARI IN THE SOUTH

To me the cuisine of India is family meals, street vendors, the love of a mother and grandmother making special dishes just for me and nuances like special meals for sons-in-law and guests. Eating in India, like any other country, is filled with its own traditions. Traditions, rituals and family and friends bind us and give us meaning in life. Many traditions have changed or evolved over the years. For example, now family-style serving has become very popular in middle- and upper-class families, and it also means everyone eats together. Even among all these changes you still see tradition and love well preserved.

When I came to United States after my marriage, the first thing I looked for was the availability of spices and ingredients to make traditional meals at home. I was able to get most of everything except a few tropical fruits and vegetables. Many things that I had always eaten when dining out I learned to cook at home. Over the years the availability of ingredients has increased tremendously especially since about 1990. Even so, when I visit India all I say is, "Oh my, I haven't eaten this in years."

In this country the common question I hear is, "Isn't curry Indian?" My initial reaction was to ask, "What is *curry*?" And I was totally disappointed to learn that people called curry anything that was yellow and cooked with curry powder. So people either liked or totally disliked "curry," and therefore, they either liked or disliked Indian food.

Curry is a word concocted by the British who probably wanted a one-word answer to describe the Indian cuisine. There is a word in Indian languages, *tari*, which means "sauce" or "gravy." What ever the reason or cause behind it, *curry* stuck and has become synonymous with Indian cuisine. It is a new word of the last three to four decades of the twentieth century and has become part of our vocabulary. All that is fine;

after all that is how languages evolve. The problem is the use of curry powder, a blend of spices that when added to meat or vegetables creates a yellow and spicy dish called "curry." Indian cooks have a problem with curry powder; it is not only a simplistic approach but an injustice to the cuisine. Most Indians don't own a bottle of curry powder, because they take pride in making each dish with its own unique blend of spices.

Indian cuisine is a conglomerate of regional cuisines with varying culinary characteristics. The regional variations are based on climate, availability, culture and religion. The cuisine of India can be broadly divided into five regions: north, south, east, west and central. Each region has its own specialties and peculiarities. The variation is not only in the main ingredients but also in the method of preparation, the spices and the medium of cooking.

India is home to several religions. The predominant religions are Hindu, Muslim, Sikh and Christian. The Muslim influence came around the sixteenth century with the establishment of the Mughal Empire. Muslims gave India *tandoori* breads and meats. The result is the mughalai cuisine that is very popular in north India. This type of cooking in India has evolved over the years, creating a mughalai cuisine that is uniquely Indian.

The bread introduced by the British became a major part of the Indian diet. We call it *double roti*. You will find the traditional loaf of bread as well as a variety of spiced Indian versions. Tea, in its present form, was popularized by the British. It is served with milk and sugar as *chai* and has been known as an Indian drink for years.

Another foreign influence was from the Parsees, who came from Persia and settled in Mumbai and Gujarat. The food eaten in those areas has a lot of Parsee influence.

As each new wave of settlers arrived in India, they brought with them their own culinary practices, and over the years, they adopted some of the Indian ways. Often the food was Indianized, and what resulted was a fusion of flavors that has become part of Indian life. Indian cuisine has been enriched by all the migration and culinary influences.

India is predominantly Hindu. Millions of Hindus, Sikhs, Jains and Buddhists are vegetarian. It is difficult to truly document when the vegetarian movement began to take shape. Vegetarianism might have been influenced and popularized by the Buddhist and Jain movements, two major religions that preached *ahimsa*, or nonviolence. As early as the fifth century B.C.E., Hindu scriptures prohibited meat. However, it is among the Brahamins, the priestly class, that the forbiddance of meat eating was most rigorously enforced. People of other castes sometimes accepted vegetarianism either through religious persuasion or economic necessity. Not all Hindus are vegetarians, but Hindus do not eat beef and Muslims do not eat pork.

The vegetarian tradition in India is widespread. How many people are true vegetarians is basically a guess. Most Indian vegetarians use milk products; so they are lacto-vegetarians. There are people who live in the coastal region and call fish the "fruit of the ocean." They consider themselves vegetarians even though they include milk and fish in their diet. During the last two to three decades of the twentieth century, unfertilized eggs have been sold as vegetarian eggs, so some people are lacto-ovo-vegetarians. Even the nonvegetarian Hindus and Sikhs do not eat meat during any auspicious or religious occasion.

The variety in vegetarian dishes is unique to Indian meals. Beans, lentils, milk and nuts provide the protein in the diet. A typical Indian vegetarian meal consists of *dal* (pulses), *roti* and/or rice, vegetables and yogurt. The meal is often accompanied by relishes, *papad*, chutneys and pickles. Wholesome Indian meals are expertly mixed to provide complete protein as well as vital minerals and vitamins.

According to Indian scriptures, food is divided into three categories based on its qualities. *Satvik* food is light, bland, usually vegetarian and white and gold in color. Grains, *ghee*, milk, yogurt, honey and fruits are the foods of ascetics. *Rajasic* food, suited for kings and warriors, is gold and red in color. It consists of meat, fish, eggs, wine and beer (in moderation) and is considered to be passion arousing. *Tamasic* food is red and black in color and consists of the flesh of small animals, pork and beef, scaleless fish and food cooked the day before. These definitions are often used in Ayurvedic medicine or treatments. The categories are sometimes referred to when describing the type of food eaten or even prohibited.

Festivals

Indians love to celebrate. There are so many festivals that it is impossible to keep track of them. Some are regional festivals, and others are celebrated throughout the country. They may be inspired by the harvest season, or a seasonal change, but most are religious in nature. All Indians do not celebrate every festival. The national holidays are few and represent the main holidays from each major religion. An essential part of the celebration is feasting, rituals or offering food to God. There are certain dishes and preparations that are attached to particular festivals. The dish associated with the festival is usually a regional, family or a religious tradition. For example in the north to celebrate a special occasion, *laddoos* (a dessert) are important; in Gujarat it is invariably *pedas* (a milk dessert); and in the south it is often *paisum* (pudding). Festivals break the day-to-day routine and bring color and fun to life.

Spices

The art of Indian cooking lies in the subtle use of spices. To a Westerner spicy food often translates as chile pepper hot but to an Indian spicy means layers of spices that enhance the flavor of food. Food without spices is often characterized as bland food made for a sick person. Spices are essential to Indian cooking. Indian kitchens are usually equipped with thirty or more spices and their blends. We take great pride in our spice blends. When talking to Indians you will often hear "I use my mother's *garam masala,* or this is my mother-in-law's *sambhar* powder, she makes the best. To get the right flavor you have to start with the right spices and blends. The dish could be flavored with two or three spices or as many as eight to ten spices without any difficulty. What difference does it make as long as you have all the spices? To an Indian cook it takes the same amount of time or effort to add one or ten spices; it all depends on the dish, and what you are trying to get out of it. You will often hear two cooks sharing a recipe saying the secret to my dish is a pinch of a certain spice. A pinch or a dash of spice can alter the flavor and taste of the dish, and an Indian cook understands the subtlety of these spices. To learn the use of these spices is not hard or complicated, it's just a learned art that is passed from generation to generation. I learned to cook from my mother and she from her mother. The quality of a good cook or a good dish is in mastering the spices. So you can understand how appalling the thought of a store-bought curry powder can be to an Indian cook. And to think you would use the same curry powder for every dish! One blend of spices will create only one kind of dish with one flavor.

Importance of Food Temperature

Along with the taste of food and spices, the temperature of food is very important to most Indians. They take special pride in serving food piping hot. Whether it is *roti* fresh off the *tava* (griddle), steaming hot *idli* or *garam, garam chai* (hot, hot tea), hot food has a special connotation. Indians frown on lukewarm food. A common statement heard is to eat fast before the food gets cold (not to be confused with eating too fast). Indians feel that hot food is more appetizing and better digested.

Evolution of the Indian Kitchen

In India the kitchen is the center point of a home as it is in most other countries. I have seen Indian kitchens change dramatically over the years. When I was young in the early 1960s cooking was done sitting down. All kitchens were equipped with a *chullah,* an earthen fireplace for cooking. It used firewood and most of the cooking was done on the open fire. The women sat near the floor on a wooden stool about six inches high and cooked on this fireplace. There is a saying *"chullah chad gaya,"* which means "the cooking has started." Then came the coal, and the *ungeethi* (coal stove) was born. Initially, the coal stove was used occasionally and the earthen fireplace was the main source of cooking. Over time the coal stove became very popular because coal holds heat longer and creates less smoke. The earthen fireplace became extinct in most middle- and upper-class families. The poor people still used the earthen fireplaces but some also used coal stoves. Then came kerosene and kerosene stoves. These stoves quickly became common and along with them another transformation took place.

Counters were installed in kitchens and the cooking was done standing. Then came the gas stoves and slowly the coal stoves also became extinct or were used only for special cooking. Now even villagers have gas cylinders and stoves and gradually the cooking has moved to standing. Traditionally, when the cooking was done sitting, the kitchen was a sacred place and one could not walk into the kitchen wearing street shoes. There were special wooden shoes for the kitchen. In most houses these traditions are still followed. If one enters the kitchen, shoes are left outside. This is to maintain the cleanliness of the kitchen, which Indians take very seriously. Today for many families with a standing kitchen and other ways of maintaining hygiene and food safety, such as refrigeration, shoes in the kitchen are no longer a taboo. But don't ever assume anything in India, look for signs to see what is acceptable in the family. It is safer to be too traditional than too modern.

Along with the standing kitchens came other changes. Traditionally, when mothers cooked while sitting on the floor, people also sat on the floor and ate. It was very common for the family to sit next to the mother in the kitchen and eat piping hot food as she prepared it fresh. Can you imagine a hot *roti* brought straight from the stove to your plate to your mouth? Eventually, as the cooking moved off the floor so did the eaters. In most families, people now eat at the table. The table is typically near the kitchen and hot food has equal importance. Some people may argue that something is lost in the process but I beg to differ. Modernization has helped women tremendously without taking anything significant away from the meals. Family values and eating together are well instilled in India whether they eat at the table or on the floor.

Dining Etiquette

Traditionally the food was served in an individual *thaali* (metal plate) from the kitchen. With eating at the table came family-style serving. This allows each person to serve himself and saves trips back and forth for the cook or the server. As the number of people in the family decreased it became more practical. When serving yourself there are strict rules you must follow. You must use only your left hand to serve yourself. You should touch only what you intend to take and your left hand must be kept clean at all times. There is a great sense of *jhoota*, or polluting the food. It is important to maintain hygiene, although older people can be quite neurotic about it. It made sense for them, because this was their way of keeping food safe for the family.

Indians eat with their hands. The right hand is used for eating and the left hand is used for picking up the glass of water and taking food. North Indians use only the tips of their fingers for eating. The south Indians use their whole hand, as they deem necessary. Spoons, forks and knives are considered modern utensils. North Indians use their hands to eat *roti* and now use a spoon to eat rice and other liquid foods. South Indians are experts in eating everything with the hand and use a spoon or fork only in formal situations. Eating with the hands takes a little getting used to—like chopsticks. If you don't want to eat by hand, feel free to ask for a spoon, fork and knife, because they are totally acceptable.

Meals and Snacks

Lunch is usually eaten around 1:00 P.M. and it is typically the main meal of the day. After that is siesta time. If the situation permits, Indians never miss an afternoon nap. Around 5:00 P.M. is teatime. Children are served milk or *sherbut* (sugared, flavored beverage) while adults drink tea and eat fried spicy snacks. India is the home of a variety of salty and spicy hot snacks that have no equivalents in other cultures. This is often the time friends visit to share snacks and gossip or to discuss the news of the day. The more important or rare the friend, the greater the number of snacks served. Indians take pride in serving a number of dishes at meals or teatime.

Even after more than twenty years in the United States, I really miss a good snack when I go shopping. I will often say, "I wish there were someone selling *samosa* and *chai*." You can find coffee and even *chai* now but all the snacks served with it are typically sweet. In India, snacks are abundant. *Chat, samose, dahi bade* and *pakore* are commonly sold on the street. The best part of going shopping is to stop and have a plate of *chat* on the way back home. As I am writing this, my mouth is watering as I am thinking of the hot and spicy taste of *samosas* with tangy hot chutney sold at the corner shop. You don't snack to fill your stomach but to make your mouth and taste buds come alive. I never remember it ruining my dinner. The street foods of India are unique. With *pani puri* in the north, *bhel* in Mumbai and *bhaji* in the south, the street foods are part of the Indian culinary world.

One thing is clear—Indians love to eat. The surest way to go down memory lane is to have a food remind you of your aunt or grandma or that place you visited and had the best dish ever. Whenever I have friends over for dinner we eat food, talk about food, share recipes and share memories of food and relationships. Over the years my friends have shared numerous recipes and memories and I came to realize how we hold food near and dear to our heart. My children when visiting India are sometimes frustrated with all the attention their eating gets from family and friends. After all we may visit two to four families in one day. As they have gotten older they have come to accept and enjoy the process.

Restaurants

Street vendors and restaurant dining became popular only in the 1960s as people traveled and became more adventurous. Dining in restaurants was initially started by the Punjabies. The meals served at these restaurants came to be known as Punjabi or north Indian food. This menu became the formula of success. Most restaurants worldwide now serve a similar menu, which has come to be known as "Indian" food. Home-style cooking is hardly ever served in the restaurants, giving one a limited view of Indian cuisine. To enjoy the best Indian cuisine and its true diverse nature is to experience home cooking.

To experiment with exciting and new foods is one of the delights of living. Indian cuisine offers a variety of dishes that are sure to please any palate. The art of Indian cooking is easy to learn because it requires few very basic skills, and the rest is a good guide and a desire and willingness to learn.

NORTH INDIA
THE MUGHALAI INFLUENCE

Jammu and Kashmir, Himachal Pradesh, Punjab, Haryana and Delhi are the northern states of India. North India is blessed with fertile land. Wheat is the staple food and predominant crop of this region. Basmati rice, a long-grain aromatic rice, is grown in the northern plains. It is more expensive than other varieties of rice and, therefore, is used for special dishes and occasions. Rice in the northern states became more popular after independence from the British.

The northerners also consume a large variety of *dals* (beans and legumes) such as chickpeas, kidney beans, and black gram (*urad dal*) as well as *moong* and *toor dal* (pigeon peas). The use of butter, milk and *ghee* (clarified butter) is very popular. Most of the cooking is done on the stovetop using the roasting and frying method. The use of the *tandoor* (clay oven) is limited to restaurant cooking or some Punjabi homes.

Delhi, the capital of India, is a busy place. It is a mix of old and new. There is the Kutub Minar, Lal Kila, (Red Fort), museums, national monuments, parks, traffic, people and shopping galore. One of my favorite places in Delhi is the Red Fort. I took my first tour of the Red Fort when I was a young girl. As the tour guide showed us the fort, he reiterated stories of the kings and queens. My favorite imagery is of the queens shopping in the Red Fort bazaar as all the fineries of the world came to them. The government now supports small handicraft shops at the entrance of the Red Fort. I get a little nostalgic when I shop there. In front of the Red Fort is the Mina Bazaar. It used to be the most famous bazaar of its time. It is still popular for gold and silver jewelry.

Delhi is full of Indian history. It has been ruled and invaded since the Vedic times, but now Delhi is truly cosmopolitan. Here people of all races, cultures and traditions can be found. Most new things start from Delhi and that applies to food also. You can find all kinds of food there from all over India and the world. People of Delhi are used to new foods, as new settlers come to Delhi all the time. The food there was influenced by the Muslim invaders and later the British colonizers. After independence, because of the large-scale migration from Pakistan, the Punjabi influence increased. As the mobility of Indians grew, came *idli-dosa* (rice dishes) of south India. Recently Chinese and American foods have gained popularity. Fast food has been part of Delhi for a long time but it was mostly served by street vendors. Now fast food and chain restaurants are popping up everywhere. The most popular fast-food restaurants are the ones that serve a variety of foods. There is one called Nirula, where you can order *chole bature* (spicy chickpeas with fried bread), a Punjabi specialty; *dosa* or *idli*, a south Indian specialty; or *bhel* (snack mix with chutneys), a Mumbai specialty. And you can order pizza, vegetable or lamb burgers or chow mein, topping it all off with rose or chocolate ice cream. Don't be too surprised to find pizza with pickled cauliflower or chow mein that is too sweet and spicy as most foods have been Indianized. This is equivalent to an Americanized version of pizza or tacos. You can find the best snacks, sweets and restaurants in Delhi. Feast your fancy; enjoy a small corner shop or a five-star hotel. You are seconds away from a memorable culinary experience. Over the years Delhiets have created a cuisine of their own, in which national and international foods are prepared in the same household.

North of Delhi is Harayana and Punjab. These two states were separated in 1967, language being the main reason for division. Haryana is predominantly Hindu and the language spoken is Hindi. Punjab has more Sikhs and the language spoken is Punjabi. These are agricultural areas. The food of these two states is quite similar. The food is typically referred to as Punjabi food. Their best known dishes are *saag* (mustard mixed with other greens) and *makki-ki-roti* (*roti* made of corn flour). The food and culture in this region is greatly influenced by the Muslims.

After independence from Britain and the India-Pakistan partition, the culture of this area changed significantly. Masses of Punjabis, refugees from West Punjab, which now is in Pakistan, came and settled in Punjab, Haryana and Delhi. These were very enterprising people, who had style and food of their own. Slowly these refugees changed the market scene of this region by opening shops and restaurants where traditionally the *baniya* (business community) did business. I remember standing in a marketplace in Ambala Cantt (in Haryana) and my uncle said, "See all these shops, they were mostly owned by the Agarwals (*baniyas*), and now in just a short twenty years the Punjabis have taken over." Punjabis opened restaurants at every corner and *tandoori* food was born. They developed a formula that worked and Punjabi food became very popular. Today most Indian restaurants around the world serve *tandoori* dishes and typically Punjabi food.

Whenever I visited Haryana I enjoyed two different food experiences. When I visited my mother's home, a very orthodox family, I ate very traditional vegetarian food. A typical meal there might be *moong dal*, *subji* (vegetables) and *phulka* (thin *roti*). The food was expertly seasoned with spices. Onion and garlic were not used in many Hindu traditional dishes. The food was relatively pure and did not have Muslim or Punjabi influence.

On the other hand when I visited my father's home, which was also in Haryana (Shahabad Markanda), the food (also vegetarian) was heavily influenced by the Punjabi food. They also did not use garlic. The food there was a cross between traditional and Punjabi food. Stuffed *parathas* (pan-fried *roti*), *saag* and *makk-ki-roti* for lunch and *kofta* (fried vegetable dumplings in a sauce) and *parathas* for dinner was not unusual. I was used to this food, for this is what my mother made at home. My aunt made my father's favorite dishes and eating in this family was anything but simple. They loved extravagant and lavish meals and the women took pride in making their finest dishes.

Kashmir is predominantly Muslim and the food here is unique to the region. Himachal Pradesh's food is a happy blend of Kashmiri and Punjabi food. Many of the Hindus in Kashmir are Brahmins (the priestly class). Pandit Jawaharlal Nehru, the first prime minister of independent India descended from this region. Kashmiri Brahmins eat meat, although Brahmins typically denounce meat. They enjoy lamb cooked with asafetida, ginger, fennel seeds, ground red chiles and other spices as well as a yogurt or milk base. The Brahmins frown on onions and garlic, because they say these ingredients encourage base passion. They also eat lots of beans and vegetables. During the long hard winters dried meat and vegetables are used extensively.

The Kashmiri Muslims season their dishes with onion, garlic, ginger and other spices. The possibilities of lamb dishes are endless. Hindus don't eat beef and the Muslims are forbidden to eat pork. So lamb became the most popular meat in northern India. *Rogan josh* (lamb and yogurt dish) and *biriyani* (lamb and rice dish) come from this region. The Kashmiri breads are also unique and are not found in the rest of the country. The most popular breads here are more like Middle Eastern and Afghanistani breads and are baked by professional bakers, unlike the *roti* and *puri* of the rest of India. The Kashmiries also love rice; basmati rice is very popular, especially for *biriyani* and *pulao* (rice pilaf).

CENTRAL INDIA
GHEE, PURIES, JELABIES AND KEBABS

Rajasthan, Uttar Pradesh (UP), Madhaya Pradesh (MP) and Bihar are the central states of India. Often these states are also referred to as north India. It is best to describe this region separately, because it has its own characteristics. UP is the most populated state in India. To the north it borders the magnificent Himalayan Mountains and Nepal. Through UP flows the sacred river Ganges on its way to the Bay of Bengal. Madhya Pradesh ("central state") is the largest state in size and is geographically located in the heart of India. Bihar to the east suffers from severe droughts, although several rivers flow through it. Bihar is the home of Lord Buddha and thousands of Buddhist pilgrims journey there each year. These states, although predominantly Hindu, have pockets of Muslim settlers along with other religions. The cuisine is a combination of both Hindu and Muslim cultures. These states have many similarities in their style of cooking but there are some specialties of each state.

The Festival of Diwali

Diwali, the festival of lights, is a national holiday and is celebrated throughout India around mid-October with lots of festivities similar to Christmas in the Western world. Hindus observe Diwali for different reasons. Basically it is to celebrate the victory of good over evil and/or to welcome the goddess of wealth, Lakshmi, into one's home.

Everyone is in the holiday spirit; the homes are cleaned inside and outside. The shops are cleaned, decorated and full of goods. The most spectacular sights are the sweet shops. The *halwai* (maker of sweets) shops have lined up the sweets, five to six tiers high. There are *barfies* (diamond-shaped dessert) of all different colors, shimmering with *vark* (edible silver foil); *khoa* (evaporated milk); and *kaju-pista* (cashews-pistachios). Tri-colored *barfies* are made fresh everyday. The *rasagullas, cham-chams* (both made from fresh cheese) and a variety of *laddoos* (round sweets) are all arranged, stacked and heaped in an inviting manner. People are lined up to buy boxes of sweets to take home. The children gleefully accompany their parents to buy their favorite firecrackers. In my family, because we are five brothers and sisters, my father would always divide the firecrackers among us so we wouldn't fight. That only reduced the problem a little, as we traded, finagled and manipulated the little ones. On the day of the Diwali are the *pooja* (prayers) and cooking of the traditional Diwali meal. In my house it was always *puri* (fried puffed bread), *kachori* (stuffed fried bread), *aloo* (potatoes), *kaddu* (pumpkin) and *boondi raita* (yogurt with small balls made of chickpea flour) and lots of sweets. It is an auspicious holiday and only vegetarian fineries are cooked and served. In family businesses, new account books are started and blessed as they pray for a prosperous year, to the goddess Lakshmi. It is also the beginning of the New Year based on the Hindu calendar. Hindus throughout India light oil lamps on Diwali and distribute sweets. It is a family festival with firework displays across the country. Most of north India celebrates Diwali in a similar fashion with family variations.

Varanasi in UP (formerly called Banaras) is thought to be one of the world's oldest living cities. Like other large Indian cities, Varanasi has most religions represented. It is a holy Hindu city. Religion is big business and pilgrims from all over India congregate there. The focus is the river Ganges; it is believed if you bathe in it you can wash away all your sins. After taking a dip in the Ganges and a trip to the temple, you can eat a snack or a meal. The streets are lined with small restaurants serving their specialties. Feast on a hot fresh vegetarian meal of *puri-aloo* (fried bread with potato vegetable) or snack on *kachori-chole* (stuffed fried bread with spicy chickpeas) with hot tea or *lassi* (sweet yogurt drink). Don't forget to order a plate of fresh *jalebies* (crispy sweets filled with syrup) or *rasmalai* (made of fresh cheese and evaporated milk) for dessert. The food is served hot right out of the *karhai* (wok) into your plate. Everything is prepared fresh; you can watch the cook as he sits in front of the twenty-four- to thirty-six-inch-diameter *karhai* frying your *puries* and *jalebies* to order. The best way to eat is to be served on a *pattal* (plate made of dry leaves) and *kulhar* (earthen cup); these are disposable and, therefore, hygienic. Varanasi is also known for its *paan*, which is a betel leaf digestive condiment that is eaten after the meal. Banarasi *paan* is known to be the most exotic, mellow-tasting *paan* that melts in your mouth.

As Varanasi typifies Hindu tradition, Lucknow in UP is the hub of Muslim culture. Lucknow is known for its civility, graciousness and flowery language, Urdu. The culinary tradition here is an intermingling of the two cultures. Preparations such as *kebabs*, *biriyanis* (rice and lamb dish) and mutton *korma* (ground lamb dish) are very popular. People ask for Lucknow's *revdi* (candy coated with sesame seeds), *gajak* (sugar or jaggery sweet with sesame seeds) or Dussheri (variety of mango) by name.

Rajasthan is the desert state. On its western borders is the Pakistan province of Sindh. Rajasthan is known for its striking bold colors and costumes. In the last few decades of the twentieth century, it became the tourist spot of the country. Rajasthan is predominantly Hindu with a tradition of chivalry. The Rajputs (warrior class) were traditionally huntsmen so they developed a large repertoire for game dishes. Muslims invaded, ruled and settled in this area in the eighteenth century. Thus again the Hindu and Muslim food traditions intermingled. There are many dishes that were developed by Rajput warriors while on the run. Meats including, poultry, game and fish are marinated, skewered and grilled over live fires to make kabobs. Rajputs also enjoy a variety of alcoholic drinks, of which whiskey and gin are the most popular now.

Unlike the warrior Rajputs, the Marwari community of Rajasthan is very orthodox Hindu. It is worth mentioning here because the Marwaris have settled throughout India and the Marwari *rasoi* (kitchen) or food with its unique characteristics has its own culinary place in India. Marwaris are strictly vegetarian and even refrain from garlic and onion. Marwaris are from the *bania* or business community. Traditionally, the kitchens were treated like a sacred place. Only the cooks could enter the kitchen, and even they had to bathe and wear special, freshly washed clothes. *Thaali* is the preferred way to serve food there, because they felt the metal dishes could be cleaned better than the glass ones. Orthodox Marwaris did not eat outside food. The modern standing kitchens have challenged many of these beliefs. Changes in this community are happening at an equally fast pace as the younger generation moves away from traditional dietary limitations and they eat out of necessity as well as pleasure.

When I married into a Marwari family, I noticed many subtle differences from the UP and Punjabi foods I was familiar with. The *roti* (flat bread) was thin and folded into fourths, with a liberal layer of *ghee* between each fold. The *roti* was soft and melted in your mouth. The vegetables and *dals* were cooked in oil or *ghee* and seasoned with asafetida, cumin seeds, coriander powder and lots of red chile powder, giving the dish a deep red color. They make numerous variety of *roties* other than plain wheat ones. Some of the popular ones are *missi* (wheat and chickpea flour mixed), *bajara* (millet) and *jawar* (sorghum) *roties*. The most traditional Marwari meal is *dal-bati* (bread made of whole wheat flour similar to bagels without holes dipped in *ghee* and served with *dal*) and *churma* (whole wheat dessert). Marwaries love their sweets. Sweets are often served first, then the meal and last comes the *papad*. *Papad* indicates the end of the meal. My husband just smiled when I first served him *papad* with the meal as he proceeded to tell me that serving *papad* before the end of the meal would have been insulting to his forefathers.

As in the rest of India *paan* (betel leaf specialty) is very popular in central India. *Paan* shops are around every corner, and many homes have a *paan dan* (container for *paan* ingredients). It is considered to be a digestive aid and is usually eaten after a meal. Many adults are addicted to *paan*, especially if it has tobacco in it. *Paan* is an interesting concept. It is a betel leaf, covered first with quicklime, and then *katechu* paste, and in the center goes the betel nut pieces and variety of things like fennel seeds, cardamom pods, cloves and/or tobacco. Children and some occasional *paan* eaters may like little sugar balls, and *gulukand* (made of rose petals) in it. The *paan walah* (*paan* vendor) sits in the middle with a line of ingredients in front of him, some are his secret ingredients to which you just point and say that too. The leaf is then folded in a specific triangular shape and people stick their necks out as they stuff them into their cheeks. The *paan* turns your mouth red for a while and there is no lying if you have had some. Children are typically not allowed to eat *paan* except for special occasions or as a treat. Oh, the fun when an uncle visits and takes all the kids to the *paan* shop and you get to order it the way you like it. It was pretty annoying if you had to split a *paan* with your sibling or cousin. As a child I remember eating it like a forbidden fruit.

WEST INDIA
DHOKLA, BHEL PURI AND MUMBAI DUCK

Gujarat, Maharashtra and Goa border the Arabian Sea to the west. Gujarat is the home of Mahatma Gandhi, preacher of nonviolence, who is often referred to as father of the nation. As early as the late 1800s the Gujaratis migrated to Africa and Europe, building a wide range of business across the world. Many Gujratis own hotels and motels in the United States. Gujaratis enjoy eating a wide variety of fried snacks and tidbits. The Gujaratis eat snacks at any time of the day. They are very fond of pickles and chutneys and no meal is complete without them. They do a fair amount of frying and steaming.

The food of this region is mild compared to that of the neighboring regions. They prefer a sweet and sour taste. The Gujarati food is typically seasoned with sugar or jaggery. This is quite a contrast to the north Indian style of cooking. The food is so different that the cafeteria where I went to study in Baroda served two kinds of meals, one for the locals, and one for non-Gujratis, which they called Punjabi food. We (north Indians) would sometimes be amused, because the cooks would often add a pinch of sugar as they prepared the Punjabi food. The idea of sweetening food is so ingrained that a dish without it is incomprehensible.

The cooks make wonderful *dhokla* and *bandva* (steamed rice and bean cakes), served with coriander, coconut or tamarind chutney. The *bataka vada* (fried potato snacks), *chivras* (seasoned mixture) and *khakhras* (crackerlike bread) are some of the common snacks. They make variety of *rotis*. The millet *rotis* are very popular and are served with *ghee* and jaggery. Gujratis love sweets. One of the most popular sweets is *peda* made by evaporating milk until it is solid and then transforming it into a variety of shapes. *Peda* is served at most auspicious and special occasions.

All Gujarati-speaking people are not vegetarians. Gujarat is home to the Bohris, one of the oldest Muslim communities in India. They are among the very few communities in the country with a passion for serving soups. They serve cold soups, hot soups, soups for breakfast or any time of the day. Parsis, who came from Persia, are another Gujarati-speaking minority. Parsi food is a delicious blend of Persian and Gujarati food. One of the favorite meat dishes there is *sali jardloo murgh*, a sweet and sour Persian-style chicken and dried apricots served with crunchy potato sticks. *Kid gos* consists of large chunks of very young lamb, stewed with ground cashews and coconut milk.

Mumbai the state capital of Maharashtra is a sprawling cosmopolitan city. Mumbai is the business center of India, with perhaps the largest film industry in the world.

Immigrants of every religion, color and creed have settled there. Its inhabitants are a vibrant blend of Maharashtrians, Gujaratis, Parsis, Baghdadi Jews, Muslims and Sindhis as well as people from all over India. You will find the richest and the poorest in Mumbai. It is not uncommon to find a person from Mumbai who can speak four or five languages fluently. My Rajasthani friends from Mumbai are fluent in Marwari (their mother tongue), Hindi, Marathi, Gujarati and English. Mumbai is, in fact, an excellent place to learn about India as a whole. People say that the real place to begin to know India is in the villages, which is true in the sense that the vast majority of Indians live there. But it is in the cities, particularly Mumbai and Delhi, that you get a sense of the whole Indian experience, the sense of history, of foreign influences, of the religion distinctions, of traditions and of modern influence.

Starting around Maharashtra one could draw a line that divides the basically wheat-eating north (Kashmir is an exception) from the rice-eating south. Maharashrians pride themselves in their enormous skill in fish cookery. The coastal people eat fish cooked in a variety of ways. One of the most delicious is *patra ni macchi*—the best of the coastal fishes, smothered in fresh coriander chutney, wrapped in banana leaves and steamed. Mumbai duck, which isn't a duck at all, but the dried version of a slender, rather bony fish. It may be fried crisp and crumbled over rice as sort of relish or cooked in a sauce as a curry. It is so salty that it needs no other flavoring. Both the taste and smell take a little getting used to, but it is very popular among the locals.

Mumbai, being the home of a mixture of communities has, like Delhi, developed specialties of its own. There one finds some of the best Chinese food. One of the most exemplary sights in Mumbai is Chowpatty Beach. At sundown the place is crawling with people, walking for exercise or strolling and chatting as the children run gleefully on the beach. Before you go home you must treat yourself to a plate of *bhel puri*—a spicy snack mixture of thin, crisp chickpea flour vermicelli, raw chopped onion, green chiles, fresh chopped cilantro, tamarind chutney, boiled potatoes—the list of ingredients is endless. And to drink there is fresh coconut water—served right out of the coconut. The vendor cuts the top off of a green coconut and hands it to you with a straw in it.

Moving south one experiences the lush greenery of Goa, formally a Portuguese colony. It is roughly half Catholic and half Hindu with a very strong Portuguese influence that is carried through into the food. Few if any European dishes survive their original form, because by nature Indians do not like bland food. So the hamburger here is seasoned with onion, garlic and spices. This is the home of the famous fiery *vindaloo* curry, an exceptionally hot pork dish. From Goa come countless fish and seafood recipes.

It is also the largest grower of cashew nuts. Coconut is also used extensively in flavoring and condiments. So distinct is the taste of its dishes that they are often referred to as the "Goan curry."

SOUTH INDIA
IDLI, DOSA, COCONUT AND CHILES

Andhra Pradesh, Karnataka, Tamil Nadu and Kerala are the southern states of India. This region is often referred to as south India. The landscape, climate, history, customs and habits of the people are relatively different from north India. This part of India is lush green and is known as "the temple land," because every town, city and village has an abundance of temples, some dating as far back as one thousand years. Most of this area is tropical and has a similar temperature throughout the year. The food of this region is simple and relatively pure from foreign influences. South Indians are predominantly rice eating and there are marked and clear distinctions from their north counterparts in the spices and seasonings used.

The Brahmins (the priestly class) in south India are devout Hindus. Most of the Brahmins there are vegetarian. These four states share a common heritage of foods, especially vegetarian food. There are, of course, many area specialties. Rice is the staple and no meal is complete without it. Rice is eaten three or more times a day. Extraordinary numbers of rice dishes are prepared. This may be compared to the variety of pasta dishes prepared in the Western world. The types of rice used here are round grain rice, polished rice, partly husked and parboiled rice, semiglutinous rice and basmati and other long-grain rice. Besides the variety of rice available, there is pounded rice, puffed rice and rice flour. Rice, legumes, vegetables, yogurt, buttermilk and coconut make up the core of the diet. With grinding, pounding, fermenting, steaming, poaching and frying, these ingredients are transformed into the most amazing assortment of dishes.

The most popular south Indian dishes throughout India and in restaurants around the world are *dosa* and *idli*. They are made from rice and *urad dal* (black gram *dal*), which are soaked, ground and fermented. *Dosa* which is thin like a crepe, is cooked on a hot *tava* (griddle) and served plain or stuffed with a potato and onion mixture. The stuffed version is called *masala dosa. Idlies* are made in a special container that makes twelve to sixteen *idlies* at a time. *Idlies* are steamed. Both are served with coconut chutney and a spicy *sambhar*, which is made of *toor dal* (pigeon peas) and vegetables. These are the breads of the south. They are as easily digested, due to the fermentation process, as they are nutritious and delicious. And, of course, to finish the meal there is always plain rice served with plain yogurt, pickles and *papad* (*pappadam* as it is called here). *Rasam* is also a very popular, distinctive dish of south India. It is a brothlike soup containing *toor dal* (pigeon peas) and vegetables. It is typically very spicy hot. I have had *rasam* at the home of my friend from Karnataka that opened up my sinuses. The food in most of the south is very hot and spiced with lots of red chiles. South Indians compare and guard their *sambhar* or *rasam* powder recipes as north Indians do their *garam masala* recipe.

The seasonings and spices used in this part of the country are unique to this region. The food is seasoned and garnished with mustard seeds, curry leaves, tamarind and coconut. Because they are coastal states, coconut is used abundantly. They also use *urad* and *chana dal* as seasonings, which impart their own flavors and tastes to the food. Traditionally, coconut oil was used for cooking, but as Indians became aware of dietary cholesterol, they switched to vegetable oil. *Ghee* is used mostly for flavoring and seasoning only. This is different from the north where *ghee* is given a lot of importance.

A coconut scrapper, unheard of in the north, is an absolute essential in a south Indian kitchen. It is a small device with a strong metal prong at one end. Fresh coconut is grated with this gadget everyday. Traditionally, copper cooking vessels were used, but now cooks mostly use stainless steel. Every kitchen is equipped with a steam cooker. Many items in this region are cooked over steam, a technique virtually unknown in the north.

For large celebrations, a wedding or a festival, people sit on the floor and their meals are served on a banana leaf. This is their version of disposable dishes, similar to the dried-leaf *pattals* of the north. South Indians eat with their hands, they may plunge their whole hand into the food if they so desire. Eating *rasam* with the hands takes practice. It reminds me of how the Chinese eat soup with chopsticks.

South Indians are serious coffee drinkers who generally begin by buying the green coffee beans of their choice. They are then roasted in the store or at home. It would not be unusual for a family to roast coffee beans every morning and then grind it fresh. South Indians here make strong, filtered coffee. The coffee is then mixed with lots of hot milk and sugar. My friend from Karnataka is so particular about his coffee that he freezes the roasted coffee beans and grinds them fresh in the morning. Mysore (Karnataka) coffee is famous worldwide.

Hyderabad, the capital of Andhra Pradesh, is the main Muslim stronghold in this area. The food in Hyderabad is similar to Muslim food in north India, but has an individuality all its own. It makes abundant use of fresh mint leaves and lots of lemon juice. Age-old dishes—such as *haleem* (small pieces of meat cooked with whole wheat) and the famous rich *biriyanis* (rice cooked with a mixture of spices and mutton or chicken)—are absolutely out of this world.

The coastal state of Kerala is scalloped with dazzling white sand beaches and lined with palm, cashew, guava and mango trees. Kerala is the home of black peppercorns, nutmeg, cinnamon, cloves, tamarind, cardamom, ginger, turmeric, curry leaves and coconut. These spices have lured traders into Kerala since ancient times. Devout Hindus, Muslims, Christians and Jews live in harmony there. Fish, chicken and lamb as well as beef are eaten. Perhaps owing to its high population of Christians, Muslims and Jews, beef is eaten fairly freely.

Thousands of fishing communities are found along the coastal regions, each with its own impressive and elusive characteristics. The fishing people in these communities have their own festivals and ceremonies. One of the most common dishes, *meen vala* curry (fisherman's curry), is simple, flexible and delicious. It can be made with pomfret, mullet or mackerel. The delight of this dish depends entirely on the quality and flavor of the fish. Herring, sardines, prawns, shrimp and small crabs are of an unsurpassed delectability. Dried fish is used during the monsoon season. Fish are also pickled here. The variety of curries and curryless dishes (without gravy or sauce), dried fish preparations and pickles, shellfish, freshwater and saltwater fish enjoyed here are sure to please any fish lover. The meat and fish are often cooked with tamarind paste, red chiles, ginger, garlic and coconut.

The south is changing as fast as the rest of India. The traditional Indian life and the social structure are changing. The modern facilities, availability of food, television, movies and necessities have changed things there as well. South Indians now enjoy *roti* and other north Indian foods in homes and in restaurants. *Puri-aloo* and *cholebhature* are as popular in the south as *idli-dosa* is in the north.

THE EAST
TEA, FISH AND RASAGULLA

The eastern region of India is a vast and varied area. The states of Orissa, West Begal, Assam, and several smaller states (Arunachal Pradesh, Sikkim, Nagaland, Manipur, Mizoram, Tripura and Meghalaya) make up the eastern region. With the Bay of Bengal to the south and the Himalayas to the north it has varied landscape and climates that influence the agriculture and availability of food. Countries such as Bangladesh, Nepal, Bhutan, China and Burma surround this region. There have been numerous political, geographical and social changes in this area since the 1970s. Historically, many of these states were tribal and followed tribal customs and traditions. All these changes are sure to affect the present food habits of the region. Rice is grown abundantly, hence it is the staple food of this region, and the food is as varied as the land.

The state of Orissa, with the famous temples of Konarak and Jaganathpuri, are set among rich vegetation. The food of Orissa has its own culinary characteristics, it is a mixture of that from Andhra Pradesh to the south, Madhaya Pradesh to the west and Bengal to the north. Abundant use is made of both saltwater and freshwater fish, with an endless supply of mouthwatering shellfish.

Calcutta is a cosmopolitan city in West Bengal. Calcutta has a mixed culinary history, because it existed the longest under continuous and very direct foreign rule. The Portuguese were trading there when the British arrived. The British set up trading posts under the name East India Company in Calcutta. Calcutta was the capital of British India until it was shifted to Delhi in 1912. But, the Bengalis, however Westernized, did not give up their language or their Bengali food and their passion for fish, rice and sweets.

Bengal has a rich tradition of fish cookery, as there are many rivers flowing into the area. Brahmins, the priestly class, are basically vegetarian. But the Bengali Brahmins eat fish, calling it the "fruit of the ocean," in an attempt to vegetarianize the fish or reduce the curse of eating meat. This was possibly because of historic necessity or perhaps because they could not resist the wonderful taste of fish. Most Bengalis dislike saltwater fish, feeling it lacks sweetness. An abundance of freshwater fish is available there because several rivers flow through the land. A variety of fish—perch, mullet, crab, carp, prawn, crayfish and lobster—swarm the waters. All are loved, but the people have a special place for the seasonal fish *hilsa*. It is similar to American shad in taste and texture. The most elegant of *hilsa* dishes is *elish bhapa*. Cut pieces of *hilsa* are mixed with a paste of ground mustard seeds, mustard oil, red chiles, green chiles, turmeric and salt. The combination is either wrapped in an airtight package of banana leaves or placed into a covered metal bowl and steamed. The fish stays moist and tender while allowing the spices to permeate it to the center. No meal is complete without fish and rice. Fish heads are cooked with *dal* to add richness and flavor; tiny shrimp are stir-fried with vegetables, fish are steamed, fried, smoked, made into balls and patties, even stuffed into creamy green coconuts and baked. Lamb and chicken are also very popular. The seasonings used most commonly are mustard seeds and mustard oil.

Bengalis have a great weakness for sweets. Bengali sweets are very popular all over India, especially *rasagulla* (Bengalis pronounce it "roshogulla"), *cham-cham* and *ras-malai*, all made from *paneer* (fresh cheese). Most sweets are made from milk, which is either evaporated and condensed until solid (*khoa*) or turned into fresh cheese (*paneer*). *Sandesh* (beautifully shaped sweets) and *mishti doi* (sweetened yogurt) are also very popular. Sweets are served with every meal.

Assam to the northeast needs little introduction, as anyone who loves tea will know that some of the best tea comes from this region. The people of this state are basically nonvegetarian and their food is very simple. Assamese enjoy a variety of fish as well as pigeon, duck, lamb and venison. The greenery of the state lends itself to a variety of vegetation. Fresh fruits and vegetables are abundant. One of the very popular dishes on the night before Diwali is *sag*—a mixture of fourteen different greens, lightly seasoned and stir-fried in mustard oil. Also cooked or pickled, as are many other vegetables, are *bah gaj* (bamboo shoots) and *bet gaj* (cane shoots). Numerous varieties of bananas are available, some even have seeds the size of peppercorns. All parts of the banana tree are used: the trunk, the leaves, the peel and the flesh of the fruit. Unique to this region is *khaar*, or ashes used to season food. *Khaar* is derived from burning the banana trunk and/or the banana peel. The ashes are stored in an airtight container and used as needed. *Khaar* is considered to be an alkaline, similar to baking soda but much healthier. It is thought to help with digestion. A pinch is added to vegetables or fish.

As in other regions of India, the food culture of this region is changing rapidly. As Indians cross borders for job or business opportunities and make new states their home, they share their foods with the natives; and the intermingling of flavors and textures is inevitable. All over India, people are enjoying the specialties of the north, south, east, west, and central cuisines in their homes and in restaurants.

FOOD, FAMILY AND MEMORIES

Memories of time spent with family and friends are often laden with special meals and dishes. Some of my best memories of childhood included traveling with my family to visit my grandparents. Every summer we looked forward to the trip soon after the final exams. Usually we would leave early in the morning on the 7:00 A.M. bus. All the trips were about the same but I remember this one when I was about seventeen years old very vividly.

The routine started around 5:00 A.M. Mom always made *puri* (fried bread) and *aloo* (potatoes) for the road. Everyone is running around getting ready. The whole house runs like a well-oiled machine because we are all familiar with the routine. We will first take a bus and then a train to Ambala.

At the bus stop, the shopkeepers are just stirring and following their morning routines. Only one *chai* stall is open and a few passengers are sipping tea. The bus is on time and we are on our way, we are excited and chatting with the other passengers. Then the train gate is closed for an oncoming train. As soon as our bus stops all the vendors (hawkers) flock to it. There are vendors with fresh *kakri* (cucumbers), *muli* (long white radishes) with lemon and spices sprinkled on them, there is *amrood* (guava), *chana* (roasted pulses) and *churan* (sweet and sour). The *kakri* and *muli* are the best ever, after all they are fresh picked and in season. We all lick our fingers and continue to talk to the other passengers. After the oncoming train passes we are on our way. Everyone is a little worried as we don't want to miss our train to Ambala.

As soon as we get off the bus we take a rickshaw and head to the train station. The *kuli* (the porter) tells Papa that the train is thirty minutes late, so we are okay.

The train comes and we all rush in and get our seats. The kids rush to sit by the window. Papa gets the luggage settled, after all we will be in the train for six to eight hours. Everyone is happy. Mummy and Papa are very relaxed and the children are busy looking out the window. We all get to know the other passengers in our area right away. My mother is talking to the lady next to her. They are busy sharing their life stories. Papa is reading the newspaper he bought at the station and discussing politics with the man next to him. At the next station Papa goes, and brings fresh yogurt and mangoes to be served with our lunch. By the time he comes back Mummy has spread the packed lunch on the train seat. *Puri, aloo,* yogurt and pickles and for dessert, fresh mangoes never tasted so good. Stuffed, we all rest, most passengers are now napping and the train is relatively quiet, except for the folk tunes of the beggers who entered our compartment at the last station.

At the next stop we all hear, *"Chai garam, chai garam"* ("hot tea, hot tea"), *"samose, pakore, papad, papad"* (a variety of snacks); it is around 5:00 P.M. and it's teatime. We get tea and snacks from the vendors outside the train windows. The tea is served in a *kulhar* (a disposable container made of clay), which imparts its smell and taste to the tea. I insist on *papad.* After all, this station is famous for its *papad.*

Finally we reach our destination, Ambala Cantt in the state of Haryana. We get rickshaws, I really miss the *taangas* (horse carriage) we used to take to get home, but they have basically become extinct. On the way to Nani's house we stop at the *subji mandi* (a fresh fruit and vegetable bazaar) and get a basket of fruit as a gift for the cousins.

We are greeted by our grandparents, three uncles and their families, fifteen in all. It's late and time for dinner. The women are bustling in the kitchen to cook even more dishes for us. Cousins are rushed to the nearby *halwai* (sweet shop) for dessert and three more items are added to the menu. Papa's meal is special; it is served in a *thaali* (rimmed large metal plate, typically stainless steel) lined with five *katories* (metal bowls) filled with dal, two vegetables, yogurt, and dessert. In the middle is *puri,* and on the side in a separate plate are *papad,* chutney and pickles. Only he and one of the uncles eat while two of my other uncles keep them company. That is typical, because as the daughter's or sister's husband, Papa is special. All the kids eat together, and all the women eat together at the end. It's one big party.

Papa leaves the next day and will come back after ten days to pick us up. We are having a ball with cousins, uncles, aunts, Grandma and Grandpa. We grew up in a nuclear family and this is a joint family with many activities going on all the time. We live in a small university town where hawkers are confined to the marketplace. This is a big city and vendors come to you all day long. In the morning the several *subji wallahs* (vegetable vendors) come announcing their goods. My aunt buys vegetables from them fresh every day. My cousin and I are sitting outside in the verandah with my *nani.* The next thing we know somebody brings a big *thaali* of vegetables to cut. We cut, and munch as well, on some raw vegetables as Nani tells us stories.

Around 4:00 P.M. comes the *khomcha wallahs* (snack vendors). As we are waking up from our nap we hear *"Pani puri, dahi bada,"* we look at our uncle, he calls the vendor to come and serve us. We are still savoring the hot and sour taste of the *pani puries* and here comes the *kulfi wallah* (ice cream vendor), we all get *kulfi* on a stick. I wonder how they time this so perfectly.

Today is Tuesday and one of my uncles buys special *prasad* (communion), sold only on Tuesdays, for the god *Hanuman* (the monkey god). We all go to the temple with him, after praying and offering to the god, we all get *prasad*. This is all part of being with my mother's side of the family.

The next day there is a wedding in the extended family and we are all invited. Weddings in India can go on for several days with festivities and rituals. It's a tradition to serve rice and *kaddi* (curry dish) that day. We are all seated in a line on the floor and one of the women of the house brings a large *pattal* (a plate made of dry leaves) and the water is served in the *kulhad*—these are both disposable and equivalent to today's paper products. As you are served, you use your right hand over the plate to indicate that's enough. You eat until you are stuffed, because the hosts keep coming and insisting you eat a little more. There may be plenty of servants or hired help, but on special occasions like these, family members always serve their invited guests.

My *nanaji* (grandfather) gives all the younger children twenty-five *paisa* (cents) each day and they all run to the nearby *paan wallah* (cigarette and beetle leaf vendor) and buy a variety of hard candies. I also go with them although I no longer get the twenty-five *paisa* and buy my favorite orange candies, shaped like orange segments.

In these ten days we have done all the things we love to do. But of all the things my favorite memories are of the many vendors, going to the temple, and my aunts and *Nani* making my favorite foods. I also remember spending endless hours sharing stories with my cousins and the endless teasing of my uncles.

INTRODUCTION TO INDIAN COOKING

𝄪𝄪

Indian cuisine is unique in its methods of preparation. Most Indian cooking is done on the stovetop, using direct heat. A clay underground oven (*tandoor*) is used for some cooking in the Punjab region. A gas or electric oven can be substituted for the *tandoor*.

Basic Indian food is a blend of spices, seasonings and flavorings to bring out the unique taste, flavor and aroma of each food. Because of all the types of spice (whole, ground or roasted) and the methods of preparation (roasting, in a sauce or fried) the array of possible foods is endless. When our friends get together to eat, the conversation often turns to food. I am always amazed at how many different ways we prepare the same vegetable. My friends from east or south India will often prepare the same vegetable with a totally different medium than people from the north. The combining of different vegetables or *dals* will also change the taste or texture of food.

Curry is often misinterpreted to be anything that looks yellow or resembles Indian food. The so-called curry to me is the gravy or the sauce the food is in. We call it *rasa*. Flour is rarely used as a thickener in Indian cooking. Spices, garlic, onion, yogurt or tomatoes are used to flavor and thicken the sauce. All Indian foods are not in a curry sauce; many foods are spiced yet have no liquid.

COMMON METHODS OF PREPARATION

Roasting (bhun-na): Roasting or browning of spices and food is another very common method of bringing out the taste and flavor. The food or spices may be dry-roasted or roasted in hot oil. *For dry-roasting*, heat the ingredients in a heavy frying pan over low to medium-high heat, stirring or shaking the pan occasionally. This roasting procedure brings out the flavor of the spice. For example cumin seeds are dry-roasted and ground for seasoning uncooked food, like yogurt. *For roasting in oil*, spices are added to hot oil and browned before other ingredients are added for cooking. They may also be added to this seasoned oil and browned before the water is added to make the sauce. I remember my mother saying the more you *"bhuno"* it, the better the flavor.

Seasoning (chounk): This is the most common way to season the food. Oil or *ghee* is heated until it is very hot and a slight film develops over the oil. Spices like cumin or mustard seeds are dropped into the hot oil and cooked for only a few seconds until the seeds begin to brown, pop or change color. This seasoned oil is the *chounk*. One may add the hot seasoned oil to the food or add the food to the seasoned oil. The *chounk* enhances the flavor of the spices and the food.

Thickening the sauce (tari): If the sauce is too thin, remove the lid of the pan, increase the heat and allow the liquid to evaporate to the desired consistency. This is often done to create the sauce of desired consistency. Actually thickening also adds to the flavor of the dish. When preparing a dry vegetable dish (*sukhi subji*), there will be some water in the vegetables. Once the vegetables are cooked to the desired tenderness, the liquid is evaporated and the spices cling to the food.

Adding yogurt to masala: Yogurt is added to many sauces to give them a creamy texture and to thicken and add a slight tartness to the food. Yogurt curdles when it is heated. To avoid curdling, lightly whip the yogurt to break any lumps. Add one tablespoon at a time to the browning sauce or *masala*. Fry or roast the *masala* until the yogurt is fully absorbed before adding the next tablespoon.

Simmering: According to its definition, simmering means cooking food in a liquid that boils on low heat. In Indian cooking food is often simmered on low to medium heat and liquid may or may not be added. For example vegetables may be simmered until tender without adding any liquid. Vegetables are cooked in their own juices, and once the vegetables are seasoned and heated thoroughly, the juices are released, which becomes the medium for simmering or cooking.

Reducing the fat: As mentioned earlier the spices and food are seasoned and roasted in oil. To maintain the authentic flavor and texture of food, start with roasting the spices in a very small amount of oil. Then add the food and roast it if needed. (Using a nonstick pan helps if more roasting is to be done.) Once the food is cooked, remove the lid and reduce the sauce to the desired consistency. For foods with sauce, there is no need to add more oil. For dry vegetables that have to be roasted in oil, first cook the vegetables and evaporate the liquid, if any. Then add a small amount of oil and roast some more to bring out the desired full flavor and texture. The total amount of fat in the prepared dish will be significantly less than the original recipe without compromising any of the taste.

KITCHEN EQUIPMENT

Indian cooking does not take any special utensils. If you have a well-equipped kitchen you may not need anything special for authentic Indian cooking.

The equipment listed below helps save time, energy and fat in cooking.

Blender: A sufficiently powerful blender is very useful for grinding all kinds of spices. In earlier days, people used different types of stones for grinding.

Coffee grinder: The coffee grinder is the most effective method of grinding spices in seconds. It grinds them finer than a blender, although a blender can be used followed by a sieve. To avoid any problem of a spice smell lingering in the coffee grinder, wipe it clean immediately.

Food processor or dough maker: A food processor is very helpful for grinding some *dals* and grains. I find a food processor or dough maker most useful for making all types of dough for a variety of Indian breads.

Electric food chopper: Although not necessary, it is nice for chopping onions, ginger or chiles in large quantities.

Electric rice cooker: If you frequently cook large quantities of rice, the electric rice cooker is useful. Rice is not cooked any faster in a rice cooker but it is convenient to use and makes cooking foolproof.

Heavy skillets, pots and pans: Indian cooking requires browning (*bhun-na*) and seasoning (*chounk*) over direct heat. A pan with a heavy bottom that allows for even cooking and can withstand long periods of heating is best suited for Indian cooking.

Iron skillet or tava: A cast-iron, slightly rounded or flat, surface is best for cooking *roti* (bread). It maintains temperature and allows for even cooking. A heavy frying pan can be substituted for a *tava*, which is a flat cast-iron griddle.

Nonstick frying pans: Heavy nonstick frying pans require less oil or fat for cooking. They are irreplaceable in the kitchen. Take care to prevent ruining the finish. A good combination is a small (six-inch) one and a large (ten-inch) one with lids; they're great for all types of cooking, especially vegetables.

Pressure cooker: A pressure cooker saves time and energy. It is irreplaceable for cooking beans. See "Using the Pressure Cooker" (page 30) for some tips.

Wok or karhai: An Indian *karhai* is similar to a wok. It is used mainly for frying and some roasting or browning. The *karhai* is usually small and made of heavy material, often cast iron. If you do not have a *karhai*, a wok or a frying pan can be substituted. A *karhai* needs less oil than a deep-fat fryer. An electric wok is not suitable for most Indian frying, although the electric fryer can be used for some of the frying.

NO TIME TO COOK

With the busy lifestyle of the new century, who has enough time to cook elaborate meals that take hours to prepare? As a working mother, I prepare most of the meals for my family in less than one hour. Over the years, I have learned many time-saving techniques that help in getting that favorite meal on the table with minimum time. The majority of Indian cooking is done on the stovetop. With modern appliances, a stove with four burners and a little preparation, a delicious, authentic Indian meal can be prepared quickly and efficiently.

Time-Saving Tips

I am always looking for ways to cut down on cooking time. I love cooking but like to spend as little time as I can in the kitchen. Since the majority of Indian cooking is done on the stovetop, I have been known to use all four burners at once. Over the years, I have learned some prepreparation techniques and have used some time-saving devices to significantly reduce preparation and cooking time. On weekdays I like to spend no more than thirty to forty-five minutes for meal preparation. Because the evening meal is the only home-cooked meal most of us eat, this meal has to be both nutritious and satisfying.

- ◎ The most important step is to have the ingredients on hand. See Stocking the Pantry for Indian Cooking (page 32) for items to keep on hand. Indian cooking uses many dried ingredients that can be stored for a long time. For perishables I like to do my grocery shopping only once a week to save time as well as money.

- ◎ Cleaning and chopping vegetables can be time-consuming. I usually do the whole package at one time and refrigerate portions in sealed plastic bags. If you do not have time or do not like to chop vegetables, many grocery stores now carry chopped vegetables, which are convenient and quick to use. The taste of fresh vegetables cannot be duplicated; spend a little extra on fresh vegetables and taste the difference. It is well worth the money and time.

- ◎ Some frozen vegetables are a nice substitute for fresh vegetables. I especially like to use frozen green peas, French-style green beans, mixed vegetables and spinach. Keep a supply of these vegetables in your freezer.

- ◎ Do stock some canned vegetables. For a quick meal these can be very handy. I have included some recipes using canned beans and sauces.

- ◎ Keep a running grocery list and encourage family members to add items as needed. This is especially helpful if you have more than one cook in the house.

- ◎ Plan meals for the upcoming week and add the ingredients to the shopping list.

- ◎ Double the recipes and freeze the extra for those days when nobody can or wants to cook. Remember, however, that not all things freeze well.

- ◎ Have the butcher package meats in family-size packages, or divide the meat into meal-size portions and freeze them. I usually have the butcher skin the chicken and chop or grind the meat to my specifications. The butcher will also debone and trim meat. Some places charge a little extra and some will do it at no extra charge. To me it is well worth the money, because it saves a lot of time and mess.

- ◎ To skin a chicken, use a paper towel to pull the skin. If it is partially frozen it skins even easier.

◎ Buy chopped garlic and substitute it for fresh.

◎ Substitute frozen ginger for fresh. To freeze ginger, purchase two to four ounces of fresh, tender ginger. Peel and grate or chop all the ginger. To grate ginger, grate with the grain to minimize the fiber that comes out. If you have an electric chopper, finely chop the ginger and freeze it. I usually divide the ginger into approximately one teaspoon portions, placing them on a plate lined with plastic wrap and then freezing it. When it is completely frozen, remove it from the plastic wrap and store in a sealed plastic bag or container. It takes time initially but on a daily basis it saves a lot of time.

◎ Substitute frozen onion *masala*. Using the frozen Onion *Masala* (page 51) can save a significant amount of time without altering the taste of the prepared dish.

◎ Use time-saving appliances like a blender, food processor, food chopper, pressure cooker or rice cooker when possible.

To prepare meals in less than forty-five minutes, use menu items that do not take longer than thirty minutes to cook. Use these basic suggestions:

◎ Prepare the ingredients for the recipes.

◎ Start the item that takes longest to cook first. Once the item has been mixed and is now ready to simmer, move it to the back burner as it continues to cook. For a vegetarian meal I am most likely to start the *dal* in the pressure cooker first. For nonvegetarian meals, start with the meat.

◎ Start the next item and make it accordingly.

With a little practice a complete meal for four to six people can be prepared in less than forty-five minutes. Some recipes, however, take longer and should be cooked when more time is available.

Using the Pressure Cooker

After a long day at work, cooking beans can be very time-consuming, and it is virtually impossible to cook whole *dals* in time for dinner. In India, cooking with a pressure cooker is very common; it is economical and it saves fuel and time. It cooks food three to ten times faster than ordinary cooking methods. I use it to cook *dals* as well as for many other things like boiling potatoes and steaming vegetables. My personal preference is a heavy aluminum four- or six-quart pressure cooker. Here are some basic rules for pressure cooking.

◎ Follow the safety rules in the instruction manual of your pressure cooker. A pressure cooker is safe when used properly, but it can be very dangerous if the safety rules are not followed.

◎ Prepare foods according to the recipe. Be sure not to overfill the pressure cooker.

◎ Seal and place the pressure regulator on the vent pipe, if necessary.

◎ Use medium to high heat until the pressure regulator attains a gentle rocking motion or pressure is reached. The cooking time begins when the pressure regulator begins to rock gently or the pressure gauge indicates five pounds of pressure. Lower the heat to maintain a slow, steady rocking motion or to maintain the pressure level and cook for the length of time indicated in the recipe. Remember, food cooks much faster in a pressure cooker.

◎ Remove the pressure cooker from the burner. If I have time I let the pressure drop on its own by letting the pressure cooker cool at room temperature. This, of course, causes additional cooking, which is acceptable for some recipes. If the instructions state to cool cooker at once, place the cooker under running cold water until pressure is released.

◎ After the pressure has dropped completely, remove the pressure regulator, if necessary. Always remove the pressure regulator before opening the cover. Do not force the cover off. Continue cooling until the cover opens easily.

◎ Lift the cover carefully at arm's length, tilting it away from you, because some steam may escape.

◎ Again remember to follow all the safety rules and enjoy the time savings of a pressure cooker.

STOCKING THE PANTRY FOR INDIAN COOKING

Start with the ingredients for particular recipes and build the pantry up from there.

Spices and Flavorings

For detailed information, see "Spices and Other Ingredients" (page 34).

Asafetida (*heeng*)

Bay leaves (*tej patra*)

Cardamom (*elaichi*)

    Black large cardamom

    Green cardamom

Chiles (*mirch*)

    Cayenne pepper or red chile powder

    Dried whole red chiles

Cinnamon (*dal chini*)

Coconut (*nariyal*)

    Fresh coconut

    Dried coconut

Coriander (*dhania*)

    Coriander seeds

    Coriander powder

Cumin seeds (*jeera*)

    Cumin powder

    Roasted cumin powder

Curry leaves (*meetha neem*)

Fennel seeds (*saunf*)

Garam masala

Garlic (*lehsun*)

Jaggery (raw sugar; *gur*)

Mango powder (*amchur*)

Mustard seeds (*rai*)

Saffron threads (*kesar*)

Sambhar powder

Silver foil (*vark*)

Tamarind (*imli*)

Turmeric (*haldi*)

Dals

For detailed information, see the chapter Dals (page 105).

Bengal gram (*chana dal*)

Black-eyed peas (*lobhia*)

Black gram whole (*sabut urad*)

    Dehusked (*dhuli urad*)

Chickpeas (*kabuli chana*)

Kidney beans (*rajmah*)

Lentils (*masoor*)

Moong beans, whole (*sabut moong*)

    Split *moong*

    Dehusked *moong* (*dhuli moong dal*)

Pigeon peas (*toor dal*)

Canned Foods

Black-eyed peas

Chickpeas (garbanzo beans)

Kidney beans

Mango pulp

New potatoes

Tomato sauce

Flour, Rice and Other Foods

Basmati rice

Chickpeas flour (*besan*)

Cream of rice

Cream of wheat (*sooji*)

Long-grain rice

Red food color

White flour

Whole wheat flour or durum
    wheat flour (*atta*)

Dairy

Milk, skim or
    low fat

Plain yogurt, nonfat or
    low fat

Ricotta cheese,
    low fat

Fresh Vegetables

Bell peppers

Cauliflower

Cabbage

Celery

Chiles

Cilantro
    (fresh coriander leaves)

Cucumber

Eggplant

Ginger (*adarak*), fresh

Gourds, seasonal
    (for example, bottle
    gourd)

Green beans

Mint

Okra

Onions

Potatoes

Pumpkin and
    winter squashes

Radishes

Spinach

Tomatoes

Zucchini

Fresh Fruit

Have enough fruit to last the family for one week. Canned and dried fruits are a good substitute when or if fresh fruit is finished or not available.

Bananas	Mangoes	Seasonal fruits

Meat, Poultry and Seafood (Fresh or Frozen)

Chicken,
   Hind quarters and
     breast
   Boneless, skinless, breast
	Fish
	Lamb
	   Chops cubed
	   Ground
		Shrimp

Frozen Foods

French-style green beans Mixed vegetables	Mustard greens, chopped Peas	Spinach, chopped

Fats and Oils

Butter Ghee (clarified butter)	Margarine Olive oil	Vegetable oil of choice

Spices and Other Ingredients

Most of the ingredients and spices discussed here are available at any supermarket that carries a large selection of spices. However, certain ingredients are available only at a grocery store that carries Indian or Asian groceries. These days special ingredients are readily available in most medium to large towns, because as many Asian stores and cooperative or health food stores carry the Indian spices and dried beans. If necessary you may order by mail (see Mail-Order Sources, page 245).

Spices and their blends add a distinct flavor and taste to each dish. A recipe may call for whole or ground spice. The whole variety is usually more potent than its powdered form. Substituting the spices can alter the taste and character of the dish. If an ingredient is not available, omitting it may be the better choice.

A list of spices and other ingredients is given below along with their description and common Hindi translation.

Asafetida (heeng): A dried gum resin from the root of a plant, it has a very distinct pungent smell. It has medicinal properties that help in digestion, reduce gas formation and are beneficial in other ways. It is generally used in beans, lentils and some vegetables. Asafetida in its pure form is available as a lump. A powdered form, which is mixed with other ingredients and is easier to use, is also available. It takes only a pinch of asafetida to add a lot of flavor; yet it can be omitted from any recipe without altering the flavor significantly. Always store it in a separate airtight container.

Bay leaves (tej patra): An aromatic herb, the bay leaf is most often used whole for seasoning, although it may be ground in some spice blends.

Beans and legumes: See the chapter Dals (page 105).

Besan: See chickpea flour.

Black pepper (kali mirch): Black pepper is used extensively in Indian cooking. It is used whole and ground.

Cardamom (elaichi): There are two different types of cardamom pods used in Indian cooking: black pods and green pods. The bleached white cardamom pods are generally not used. Large black cardamom pods look like black beetles and have a deeper flavor than the green pods. I use them in my *garam masala* or whole in some recipes. If unavailable, substitute with the small green cardamom pods. Small green cardamom pods are frequently used for flavoring a variety of dishes and desserts. Crushed cardamom is often added to tea for flavor. The green pods are also used as an after-dinner breath freshener or just chewed any time for flavor. The black seeds are removed from the cardamom pods. They may be used as whole seeds in some recipes, crushed for garnishing or finely ground for flavoring.

Cayenne pepper: See chiles.

Chana dal (Bengal gram): It is used as a *dal* (see page 105) and it is also used as a seasoning in many south Indian dishes. It adds a nutty flavor and spice to make various *masalas*.

Chickpea flour (besan): This is the flour of Bengal *gram (chana dal)* and is very versatile. It can be used as a thickener, a batter or as a binding agent.

Chiles (mirch): A variety of chiles are used in Indian cooking. The chiles can range from mild to very hot. The most common chiles used in Indian cooking are cayenne peppers. You can eliminate or reduce the chiles in a recipe without compromising the taste significantly—the hotness of food is a personal preference. Green chiles *(hari mirch)* can be mild to very hot and are usually chopped and added to recipes. They can also be sliced or served whole in salads. The hottest part of the chiles is the seeds, so remove the seeds to reduce the hot taste if desired. Handle chiles carefully because they can make the skin tingle and the eyes burn. The green chiles, when fully ripe, are bright red. Cayenne pepper or dried whole red chiles *(lal mirch)* are used in Indian cooking. Typically, ground red chilies are used, because it adds a distinct hotness to food. It is sold as red chili powder in stores that carry Indian groceries or as cayenne pepper or ground red pepper in American supermarkets.

Cilantro: See coriander.

Cinnamon (dalchini): Cinnamon is used both finely ground and as sticks. The cinnamon sticks have a more pronounced flavor than ground cinnamon.

Clarified butter (ghee): Ghee has a light caramel color and a distinct aroma and taste. It is made from butter or cream. The butter is cooked until all the moisture is evaporated and the solids settle on the bottom. The solids are removed and the pure *ghee* is strained from the top. *Ghee* will keep for several months at room temperature, which probably explains its popularity in ancient times. Unlike butter, *ghee* has a high smoking point that makes it easy to cook with, especially over direct heat. *Ghee* is often used in Indian cooking. Like butter, the taste of *ghee* is unsurpassable, but it is high in saturated fat and should be used sparingly. I do not use *ghee* for most of my cooking, but I have used *ghee* for a few of the recipes because of its irreplaceable taste and flavor. *Ghee* is available in most grocery stores that carry Indian groceries, and it can also be made at home.

To make *ghee*, melt one pound of butter in a small skillet over low heat. Without stirring, gently simmer until the solids settle to the bottom and turn light brown, fifteen to twenty-five minutes. Watch frequently to avoid burning. Cool and strain through a cheesecloth or similar material. Store in an airtight container at room temperature.

Cloves (laung): Cloves have a distinct aroma. They are used as a whole spice or ground in a blend of spices like *garam masala*.

Coconut (nariyal): For many south Indian dishes, fresh coconut is used. In north

India dried coconut is more commonly used, because fresh is not readily available. Whole (fresh and dried) coconut is also used for religious and auspicious ceremonies. Presweetened coconut is not used in Indian recipes. Fresh coconut should not be moldy or cracked. Shake it to make sure it has plenty of water in it. To break a coconut, hold it over the sink in one hand and hit around the center with a hammer. As the shell cracks, the coconut water will come out. Consider saving the water. It is not used in cooking, but it is a very refreshing drink. The coconut should break into two halves. Remove the coconut meat with a butter knife. If it is too difficult to remove, put the coconut in the oven at 350F (175C) for a few minutes until the woody shell contracts and releases the coconut meat. Rinse the coconut in cold water. Now the coconut can be peeled with a peeler if needed or grated directly. I usually grate the whole coconut and freeze it. A hand grater or a food processor can be used. The frozen grated coconut thaws easily and can be used as needed. Dried coconut is usually finely grated. It is almost like sawdust. It is mostly used for desserts, but it can be substituted for fresh coconut in some recipes for convenience.

Coriander (dhania): This is one of the most common spices. Both the mature seeds and the fresh leaves are used. Coriander seeds are white to yellowish brown and slightly smaller than a peppercorn. The whole seeds are used in some recipes, but it is usually used as a finely ground powder. Coriander powder is a very commonly used spice. It adds flavor to as well as thickens curries. It is very important to have good coriander powder. When it gets too old, it loses its taste and flavor. I like to buy the seeds and grind my own coriander powder. Grind coriander seeds in a blender or a coffee grinder and store it in an airtight jar. Cilantro, or fresh coriander leaves, is an aromatic herb that looks similar to parsley but has a much more distinct flavor. It is usually sold in bunches (it is also called Chinese parsley). The leaves are used extensively in Indian dishes as garnish, as flavoring and in condiments (chutney).

Cumin seeds (jeera): These long brown seeds are used in multiple ways. The cumin seeds are the most commonly used seasoning in north Indian dishes. For maximum flavor and taste, the cumin seeds are dry-roasted or fried in oil. *Cumin powder* is the ground raw cumin seeds and it is used in some recipes as a seasoning. Cumin powder is readily available in most supermarkets. *Roasted cumin powder* are the cumin seeds roasted to a dark brown to black color, ground and then used as seasoning or garnish. The flavor and aroma of roasted cumin powder is indispensable in many dishes. For a recipe, see page 49.

Curry leaves (meetha neem): These highly aromatic leaves are used as seasoning for many dishes from south India. Fresh or dried curry leaves are now available in the United

States. The fresh leaves are generally sold on the stem; pull the leaves off the stem just before using to maintain the maximum flavor. If the fresh ones are not available, you can use the dried ones, although they have less flavor.

Dal: See the chapter Dals (page 105).

Fennel seeds (saunf): These are long, yellowish brown seeds that are used whole, crushed or ground. They have a mild flavor that lingers. Fennel seals are often eaten as a breath freshener or a digestive aid.

Fenugreek seeds (methi): These small reddish brown seeds have a pleasantly bitter flavor. They also have a strong, sweetish smell similar to that of burnt sugar. It takes just a few fenugreek seeds to add a lot of flavor to any prepared dish.

Flour (atta): See the chapter Indian Breads (page 75).

Garam masala: Garam masala is a blend of dried spices that is combined and ground together for use as a seasoning. *Garam masala* has its own unique flavors, depending on the combination of spices used. There are a variety of *garam masala* recipes available. It can be a potent spice blend that can alter the taste of a recipe significantly. I like to grind my own. It lasts for a long time if it is stored in an airtight container. Often cooks or families will have their own personal recipe for this blend of spices. My family recipe for *garam masala* is provided for you on page 48. You can also buy prepared *garam masala*.

Ghee: See clarified butter.

Ginger (adarak): Fresh ginger is used in many dishes for its mildly pungent flavor. It is also believed to help in digestion and is, therefore, used in many bean and vegetable recipes. Dried ginger (*sonth*) is also used, most often in some blend of spices like *garam masala*.

Jaggery (gur): Jaggery is raw sugar most commonly made from the juices of sugar cane. If jaggery is not available, you can substitute dark brown sugar.

Mango powder (amchur): This powder is made from dried unripe sour mangoes. *Amchur* adds a sweet-sourness to food. If unavailable, substitute lemon or lime juice.

Mango pulp: Canned mango pulp or mangoes are available at most grocery stores that carry Indian groceries. Mango pulp is made from a variety of mangoes. My personal favorite for shakes and ice cream is one made using the Alfanso mango. Besides the convenience, the flavor and taste of mango pulp is usually good. In season when good mangoes are available, use them for shakes if desired.

Masala: *Masala* means "spices." The word *masala* is used very loosely. It might refer to one spice, a blend of spices, (for example, *garam masala*) or a blend of spices and other seasonings that are ground together to provide the base for many Indian sauces, (for example, onion *masala*). *Masala* can be wet or dry.

Mint (pudina): This aromatic herb is often used as a flavoring. Fresh mint is used to make chutneys and added as a flavoring or garnish to many dishes like cold appetizers, drinks and yogurt dishes. Dried mint can be substituted, if necessary.

Mustard seeds (rai): Mustard seeds are the most commonly used seasoning in south Indian dishes. They are tiny, reddish brown to black seeds from a particular variety of mustard plant and smaller than the common yellow mustard seed and much less pungent. Mustard seeds are usually dry-roasted or fried in oil when used as seasoning. They are also ground and used especially in pickles.

Onion seeds (kalonji): Small black onion seeds have an earthy aroma. They are generally used for pickling. Occasionally they are used for flavoring vegetables or fish.

Red food color: Red food color is sometimes used to add distinct color to food.

Saffron threads (kesar): These are the orange-red dried stamens of a type of crocus flower, used chiefly to color food to a golden yellow. Saffron threads also contribute a mild aromatic flavor to food. Saffron is usually expensive and, therefore, used mostly in desserts or for special occasions. If saffron is not available, substitute yellow food color in desserts and turmeric in curries.

Sambhar powder: This is a blend of spices used in making *sambhar*. Like *garam masala*, families are partial to their own *sambhar* powder. See my recipe on page 50. *Sambhar* powder is available at stores that carry Indian groceries.

Silver foil (vark): Edible silver foil is used solely as a decoration on many sweets (desserts) to make them look very elegant. This is an edible shimmering foil made of pure silver. It is sold between sheets of paper and should be handled carefully. It does not add to or change the flavor or taste. It can easily be omitted from the a recipe. (Gold foil is also available, but it is rare and very expensive.)

Tamarind (imli): Tamarind is available either dried or as a concentrated liquid. It has an acidic, sweet taste. It is used to add sourness to food and is also made into condiments (chutneys). Dried tamarind is soaked in water to rehydrate it and then made into a pulp. The pulp or the juice then is used in many recipes. The concentrated tamarind is convenient, but because it is so condensed it should be used sparingly.

Turmeric (baldi): Turmeric is typically used as a powder, mainly to color food to a golden yellow. It has a mild earthy flavor and is also a digestive and an antiseptic aid.

Urad dal: This is used as *dal* (see page 106) and as a seasoning in many south Indian dishes. It imparts its own flavor and a nutlike texture to a dish. It is also mixed with spices to make various blends.

MENUS

Some menu suggestions for nonvegetarian meals, vegetarian meals and special occasions are given here. Indian meals are usually eaten with *chapati (roti)* and/or rice. *Papad*, salad, chutney, pickles, plain yogurt or *raita* are often served as condiments or side dishes. Add to your meals as desired.

Be adventurous and add one or two items to your traditional Western meals of meat and potatoes or pasta. Try Barbecued Chicken (page 156) with baked potatoes and salad or serve Cauliflower Mixed Vegetables (page 128) with spaghetti or grilled chicken with Rice Pilaf with Peas (page 92).

Nonvegetarian Menus

Tandoori Murgh
(Barbecued Chicken), page 156

Alu Matar
(Potato and Pea Curry), page 131

Piaz Aur Tamatar ka Salad
(Onion and Tomato Salad),
page 201

Naan, (*Tandoori* Bread),
page 87, or
rice

◎

Murgh Sabji Wala
(Chicken with Vegetables),
page 160

Rice

◎

Murgh Tari (Chicken Curry),
page 158

Phul Gobhi Salad (Stir-Fried
Salad), page 206

Naan (*Tandoori* Bread), page 85,
or rice

Mysore Murgh (Stir-Fried Chicken), page 168

Alu ka Raita (Yogurt with Potatoes), page 199

Salad

Roti, page 78, or rice

◎

Murgh Sag Wala (Chicken with Spinach), page 166

Tamatar Piaz ka Raita (Yogurt with Tomatoes and Onion), page 198

Rice

◎

Machhi Kali Mirch (Baked Fish with Black Pepper), page 174

Bengun (Eggplant with Tomatoes and Onion), page 140

Kheere ka Raita (Yogurt with Cucumber), page 197

Rice

◎

Machhi Aur Ghia (Fish with Bottle Gourd), page 175

Rice

◎

Sarson Wali Machhi (Fish in a Mustard Sauce), page 176

Bean-*Moong ki Subji* (French-Style Green Beans), page 147

Rice

◎

Machhi Tari (Fish Curry), page 172

Gobhi-Gajar Salad (Cabbage and Carrot Salad), page 204

Rice

◎

Tamatari Jhinga (Shrimp with Tomatoes), page 180

Sukhi Matar (Spicy Peas), page 151

Rice

◎

Gosht Kalia (Chopped Spicy Lamb), page 182

Alu Gobhi (Potatoes with Cauliflower), page 138

Roti (page 78) or Rice

◎

Alu Gosht (Lamb with Potatoes), page 192

Piaz Aur Tamatar ka Salad (Onion and Tomato Salad), page 201

Tahari (Vegetable Rice), page 94

Rogan Josh (Lamb in Yogurt Sauce), page 189

Bund Gobhi (Cabbage and Peas), page 146

Rice

◎

Madrasi Gosht (Chopped Lamb),
page 186

Palak Alu (Spinach and Potatoes),
page 134

Neembu Chawal (Lemon Rice),
page 99

❧

Kheema
(Ground Lamb with Peas),
page 184

Gobhi Gajar Ki Subji
(Cauliflower Mixed Vegetables),
page 128

Roti (page 78) or rice

Vegetarian Menus

Toor Dal (Pigeon Peas),
page 109

Gajar Ki Subji (Sweet and Sour
Carrots), page 133

Roti, page 78, or rice

❧

Masoor Dal (Lentil Soup),
page 111

Bund Gobhi (Cabbage and Peas),
page 146

Roti, page 78, or rice

❧

Chana Dal aur Lauki (*Chana Dal*
with Bottle Gourd), page 116

Bhindi Tamatar Ki Subji
(Okra with Tomatoes),
page 136

Alu ka Raita (Yogurt with
Potatoes), page 199

Roti, page 78, or rice

❧

Sprouted *Moong* (page 110)

Tamatar Piaz ka Raita
(Yogurt with Tomatoes and
Onions), page 198

Rice

❧

Gujrati Dal (Sweet and Sour *Dal*),
page 118

Bengun (Eggplant with Tomatoes
and Onions), page 140

Kheere ka Raita (Yogurt with
Cucumber), page 197

Roti, page 78, or rice

❧

Sambhar (*Toor Dal* with
Vegetables), page 122

Nariyal Chutney (Coconut
Chutney), page 213

Idli (Steamed Rice Dumplings),
page 100

❧

Nonvegetarian and Vegetarian Menus for Special Occasions

Dal Makhani (Whole Urad Dal), page 112

Bharwa Hari Mirch (Stuffed Bell Peppers), page 132

Cachumber (Tomato, Cucumber, and Onion Salad), page 202

Dhania Chutney (Cilantro Chutney), page 209

Rice or Coiled Roti, page 84

Kheer (Rice Pudding), page 217

Chole (Spicy Chickpeas), page 124

Alu Gobhi (Potatoes with Cauliflower), page 138

Piaz Aur Tamatar ka Salad (Onion and Tomato Salad), page 201

Naan (Tandoori Bread), page 85, or rice

Gajar Halwa (Carrot Sweet), page 218

Rajmah (Kidney Beans), page 114

Bhindi Tamatar ki Subji (Okra with Tomatoes), page 136

Dahi Pakori (Moong Bean Balls), page 65

Imli Chutney (Tamarind Chutney), page 211

Tandoori Roti (Oven Roti), page 77 or rice

Mango Ice Cream, page 219

Tamatari Jhinga (Shrimp with Tomatoes), page 180

Sprouted Moong, page 110

Gobhi Gajar Ki Subji (Cauliflower Mixed Vegetables), page 128

Kheere ka Raita (Yogurt with Cucumber), page 197

Basmati Chawal (Plain Rice), page 89

Nariyal Barfi (Coconut Sweets), page 222

Seekh Kebobs (Barbecued Lamb on Skewers), page 188

Bengun (Eggplant with Tomatoes and Onion), page 140

Kheere ka Raita (Yogurt with Cucumber), page 197

Pudina Chutney (Mint Chutney), page 210

Tandoori Alu Roti (Potato-stuffed Roti), page 80

Kheer (Rice Pudding), page 217

Matar Paneer (Pea and Cheese Curry), page 144

SPICE BLENDS
AND BASIC RECIPES

Here are my recipes for the *masalas* (spice blends). They are well worth the effort. Store them in a cool dry place in airtight containers and they will last several months. Good food begins with good *masala*!

Because *paneer* is so important for many Indian dishes, I have included two ways of preparing it.

GARAM MASALA

This is my mother's recipe; it probably has been developed over many generations. It is frequently used in my recipes. A coffee grinder or a blender can be used to grind the ingredients for the masala.

½ cup cumin seeds

⅓ cup whole black peppercorns

½ cup large black cardamom pods or ⅓ cup green cardamom pods

1 tablespoon whole cloves

4 cinnamon sticks

10 to 12 bay leaves

1 tablespoon dried ginger powder

In a frying pan or on an iron griddle (tava), dry-roast the cumin seeds over medium heat until reddish brown to dark brown. Cool to room temperature.

Combine all the ingredients and grind to a fine powder. Sift the spices to eliminate any chunks. Store in an airtight container.

ROASTED CUMIN POWDER

Roasting cumin seeds brings out their full flavor. The powder is used for garnishing and flavoring many dishes.

¼ cup cumin seeds

In a frying pan or on an iron griddle (tava), dry-roast the cumin seeds over medium heat until reddish-brown to dark brown. Cool to room temperature.

Grind the seeds in a blender or spice grinder. Store in airtight container.

SAMBHAR POWDER

Homemade sambhar *powder has a much fresher taste than most store-bought ones.*
You can also control the hotness of the powder by seasoning with chiles to your taste.

¼ cup chana dal

¼ cup coriander seeds

1 teaspoon brown mustard seeds

1 to 3 dried red hot chiles

¼ teaspoon fenugreek seeds

In a small frying pan, dry-roast the spices on low heat until the chana dal is reddish brown.

Cool and grind the spices to a fine powder. Store in an airtight container.

ONION MASALA

Several of the recipes call for onions to be ground and fried. Making onion masala is a time-consuming and smelly proposition. For convenience I usually make and freeze onion masala ahead of time. Once the onions are cooked the smell is reduced significantly. It takes time initially but saves a lot of time later. You'll want to use your exhaust fan when you make this masala.

> **3 pounds onions**
> **1 to 2 tablespoons water (optional)**
> **½ cup vegetable oil**

Peel the onions, cut each onion into 6 to 8 pieces. Grind the onions in a blender to a fine paste. Add 1 to 2 tablespoons of water to help the grinding process, if needed.

Pour the onion mixture into a large frying pan and cook over high heat until most of the water is evaporated, stirring occasionally. Reduce heat to medium-high. Add oil and fry onions, stirring constantly, to avoid burning. Fry until the onions are light brown. The onions will draw away from the sides of the pan into a dense mass.

Cool to room temperature. Divide the onions into about 1 tablespoon portions, place them on a plate lined with plastic wrap and freeze. When they are completely frozen, remove from the plastic wrap and store in a sealed plastic bag or container.

To use, substitute 1 tablespoon frozen onion masala for 1 small onion and 1½ tablespoons for 1 medium onion. Reduce the oil by 2 teaspoons for every 1 tablespoon of masala to compensate for the oil in the onion masala.

FRESH CHEESE
Paneer

Paneer is increasing in popularity in India. It can be combined with vegetables or made into desserts. I often make the paneer in advance and freeze it. It can be made with low-fat or whole milk, but whole milk gives the best results because it makes a creamier and firmer cheese. Low-fat milk paneer has a slightly softer texture and you may get a little less paneer than with whole milk—but you also get less fat. Nutrient analyses are given for both low-fat and whole milk paneer.

8 cups low-fat or whole milk

7 to 9 teaspoons white vinegar

2 tablespoons water

Heat the milk in a heavy 4-quart saucepan over medium heat, stirring occasionally to avoid scorching on the bottom.

In the meantime, mix 7 teaspoons of the vinegar and water and set aside. Place a large strainer over a large bowl. Line the strainer with a double layer of cheesecloth and set aside.

When the milk comes to a full boil, reduce the heat to a simmer. Gradually add the vinegar mixture to the boiling milk and stir gently. Simmer as the curds separate from the whey. If needed, add 1 to 2 teaspoons more vinegar to separate the whey and the curds. All curds are separated when the whey is greenish yellow. Remove from the heat.

Pour the entire contents into the cheesecloth-lined strainer. Discard the whey. Rinse the curds with about 2 cups cold water. Gather the cheesecloth so the curds are in the center and tie to enclose. Tie a loop in one end of the cloth and hang the curds (a kitchen cabinet door knob works well) to allow the excess liquid to drip for 30 minutes or longer. Gently squeeze the curds to remove any liquid.

Place the curds on a clean surface and mix with your hands in a kneading motion for 2 to 3 minutes. They will become crumbly. Gather together in a ball and pat into a rectangular shape about ½ inch thick. Place it back in the cheesecloth and wrap. Place between two thick stacks of paper towels and set it on a flat surface. Set a cutting board on top. Put a heavy (about 15 pounds) object on top of the cutting board to flatten the cheese. (You can use a 6- to 8-quart pan filled with water.) Let it rest for 4 to 6 hours. Unwrap the cheese and cut into ½-inch squares. Refrigerate for up to 2 days until ready to use or freeze for later use.

QUICK PANEER

MAKES 2 CUPS
OF SQUARES

PER ¼ CUP
OF SQUARES

Calories 73

Carbohydrate 3 g

Fat 4.0 g

Dietary fiber 0 g

Saturated fat 2.5 g

Protein 6 g

Cholesterol 16 mg

Sodium 66 mg

EXCHANGE

1 medium-fat meat

On days when you are in the mood for paneer and don't have time to make it from scratch, ricotta cheese can be substituted. This paneer is relatively soft. I use part-skim ricotta cheese. Just like paneer with whole milk, whole milk ricotta cheese will give you a creamier and firmer paneer. The lighter the ricotta cheese, the greater the water content. Fat-free ricotta does not make good paneer.

15 ounces part-skim ricotta cheese

Preheat oven to 350F (175C). Mix ricotta cheese with a wire whisk to blend well. Place in an 8-inch square pan.

Bake for 30 to 35 minutes, until all the liquid is evaporated and the cheese is set.

Cool completely. Cut into ½-inch squares.

BEVERAGES
AND SNACKS

ℳ Water is the beverage of choice in India. Water is served with all meals as it is cool and soothing and tastes best with all Indian foods.

Tea is served at anytime, most commonly at breakfast and teatime, which is around 5:00 P.M. A whole array of snacks are made to be served at teatime. Indians love to stop for tea and order a plate of *samosas*. There are cafes that serve many beverages such as tea, expresso coffee, *lassi* and milk shakes with snacks all day. The variety of snacks are virtually unlimited. Snacks or savories are often fried and served with chutneys. Coffee is very popular in south India.

I have included a sampling of popular snacks and beverages in this chapter. Because teatime is not as popular in the United States, I serve several of the snacks as appetizers, a side dish or a light meal. Occasionally, I serve Steamed Rice and Bean Cakes (*Dhokla*) with Sweet and Sour Cabbage (*Sambhara*), page 142, Cream of Wheat Snack (*Uppama*) with a mango shake or Potato-Stuffed Pastries (*samosas*) and *Moong* Bean Balls (*Dahi Pakari*) with yogurt as a meal.

The snacks chosen for this book are low in fat and high in taste. Enjoy them as light meals or any time of the day.

CHAI

MAKES 1
(1-CUP) SERVING

PER SERVING
Calories 11
Carbohydrate 2 g
Fat 0 g
Saturated fat 0 g
Dietary fiber 0 g
Protein 1 g
Cholesterol 0 mg
Sodium 22 mg

EXCHANGES
free

People have a passion for tea in India. Tea seems to lift the spirit at any time of the day. Teatime is 5:00 P.M. and usually includes snacks. It is an excellent way to wind up the workday. Tea in India is commonly served with milk and sugar. Spices are added, as desired, for flavor.

1 cup water

2 tablespoons skim milk

1 cardamom pod, crushed with mortar and pestle, (see Note, below)

1 teaspoon tea leaves or 1 tea bag

Sugar or artificial sweetener, to taste

Pour the water and milk into a small saucepan. Add the cardamom pod. Bring to a boil. Reduce heat to low and add tea leaves. Simmer for 1 minute. Remove from the heat. Let sit for 1 to 2 minutes.

Strain the tea into a cup. Add the sugar or artificial sweetener, if desired.

NOTE

If you make more than 1 cup of tea you don't necessarily need more spices. For example, I would add 1 cardamom pod for 1 to 3 cups of tea. The longer you let the spices boil in the water, the more the flavor will come through.

VARIATIONS

◎ Add a ¼-inch piece of fresh ginger, crushed with a rolling pin, instead of cardamom. It is especially good in the winter or when you have a cold.

◎ Some people also like cloves, cinnamon or black pepper in their tea. Use sparingly, adding to the water as other spices.

YOGURT DRINK

Lassi

Sweet lassi is a very popular drink, especially on a hot summer day. It has a mild and refreshing flavor. Serve it with snacks or with a light lunch of Pounded Rice Snack (Poha), page 68, or Cream of Wheat Snack (Uppama), page 71.

⅔ cup plain nonfat yogurt

⅔ cup cold water

1 tablespoon sugar

2 to 3 ice cubes

Place all the ingredients into a blender. Blend until frothy. Pour into a tall glass and serve immediately.

SUGAR-FREE LASSI

◎ To make sugar-free lassi substitute artificial sweetener for the sugar.

MAKES 1
(1½-CUP) SERVING

PER SERVING
Calories 130
Carbohydrate 24 g
Fat 0 g
Saturated fat 0 g
Dietary fiber 0 g
Protein 9 g
Cholesterol 3 mg
Sodium 117 mg

EXCHANGES
1 milk
½ starch

SUGAR-FREE PER SERVING
Calories 85
Carbohydrate 12 g
Fat 0 g
Saturated fat 0 g
Dietary fiber 0 g
Protein 10 g
Cholesterol 3 mg
Sodium 117 mg

EXCHANGES
1 milk

PER SERVING

Calories 85

Carbohydrate 12 g

Fat 0 g

Saturated fat 0 g

Dietary fiber 0 g

Protein 9 g

Cholesterol 3 mg

Sodium 370 mg

EXCHANGES

1 milk

SEASONED BUTTERMILK
Namkeen Lassi

Lassi is often made salty and seasoned with roasted cumin seed powder to give it a delicate flavor. It is usually made with fresh buttermilk; in India the buttermilk has a different taste and flavor. Making it with yogurt best replicates the original flavor. Enjoy it as a cool beverage anytime or serve with meals.

⅔ cup plain nonfat yogurt

⅔ cup cold water

⅛ teaspoon salt

Pinch Roasted Cumin Powder (page 49)

Place all the ingredients into a bowl and whisk. Blend until smooth. Pour into a tall glass and serve immediately.

COLD COFFEE

On hot summer days cold coffee is very refreshing. We made cold coffee after school in the summer instead of drinking milk, which was always served warm in India.

> **2 teaspoons instant coffee**
>
> **¼ cup hot water**
>
> **2 cups skim milk**
>
> **3 tablespoons sugar**
>
> **4 to 6 ice cubes**

Mix the coffee in hot water. Cool to room temperature.

In a blender, combine the cooled coffee, milk, sugar and ice cubes. Whip until frothy. Serve immediately.

SUGAR-FREE COLD COFFEE

◎ To make sugar-free cold coffee, substitute artificial sweetener for sugar.

MANGO SHAKE

MAKES 2
(1½-CUP) SERVINGS

PER SERVING
Calories 199
Carbohydrate 41 g
Fat 0 g
Saturated fat 0 g
Dietary fiber 2.4 g
Protein 9 g
Cholesterol 4 mg
Sodium 128 mg

EXCHANGES
1 milk
1 fruit
1 starch

SUGAR-FREE PER
SERVING
Calories 154
Carbohydrate 30 g
Fat 0 g
Saturated fat 0 g
Dietary fiber 2.4 g
Protein 9 g
Cholesterol 4 mg
Sodium 128 mg

EXCHANGES
1 milk
1 fruit

In India a mango shake is made with milk instead of ice cream. I remember drinking this shake in the summer when mangoes were plentiful. I use canned mango pulp here because good mangoes suited for shakes are usually not available and it is convenient and available year round. If using fresh mango, make sure it is ripe and sweet.

> **2 cups skim milk**
>
> **⅔ cup canned mango pulp or ¾ cup mango slices**
>
> **2 tablespoons sugar**
>
> **4 to 6 ice cubes**

In a blender, combine all the ingredients and whip until frothy. Serve immediately.

SUGAR-FREE MANGO SHAKE

To make a sugar-free mango shake, substitute artificial sweetener for sugar.

MAKES 1 PAPAD

PER PAPAD

Calories 35

Carbohydrate 6 g

Fat 0 g

Saturated fat 0 g

Dietary fiber 2.5 g

Protein 2.5 g

Cholesterol 0 mg

Sodium 237 mg

EXCHANGE

½ starch

BEAN WAFERS
Papad

Many varieties of papad, also known as pappadum, are available—they can be plain, mild or spicy hot. Papad can be served with a meal, very much like potato chips, or eaten as a snack. Most are made from processed dals but there are also potato and rice versions among others. The ones made with dals are the most common. If served as a snack, they are usually fried; if served with a meal, they are often roasted. I usually microwave my papad for convenience. Papad made with dal are available at stores that carry Indian groceries.

Direct fire: Roast the papad one at a time on a gas or electric stove. On an electric stove use a wire rack. On a gas stove, use tongs to hold papad. Roast papad, turning frequently to avoid burning, until it puffs.

Microwave: Place one papad on a paper towel or a microwave-safe plate. Microwave each papad for 40 to 60 seconds on high (time will vary, depending on the microwave's power). The papad will puff evenly.

VEGETABLE CUTLETS
Subji Cutlets

MAKES 12 SERVINGS
2 CUTLETS EACH

PER SERVING

Calories 103

Carbohydrate 11 g

Fat 6 g

Saturated fat 0.5 g

Dietary fiber 1 g

Protein 1 g

Cholesterol 0 mg

Sodium 282 mg

EXCHANGES

1 starch

1 fat

The word cutlet has become part of the Indian language. Cutlets are a little work but they are well worth the effort. Serve them as an appetizer, snack or a side dish. I like to eat them with Cilantro Chutney (page 209) and kids like them with ketchup.

4 medium potatoes (1½ pounds)

½ cup frozen green peas

½ cup chopped carrots, ¼-inch cubes

½ cup chopped green beans, ¼-inch pieces

1½ teaspoons salt

1 tablespoon coriander powder

½ teaspoon cayenne pepper

1 teaspoon mango powder

1 teaspoon Garam Masala (page 48) or purchased

2 tablespoons chopped cilantro leaves

¼ cup bread crumbs

⅓ cup vegetable oil

Cook the potatoes in boiling water until tender. To prevent potatoes from getting sticky, remove from boiling water as soon as they are done and cool completely.

Steam the peas and chopped vegetables until tender, about 5 minutes. Cool to room temperature.

Peel and coarsely mash the potatoes. Add the steamed vegetables, salt, coriander powder, cayenne pepper, mango powder, garam masala and chopped coriander leaves. Mix with your hands to combine.

Shape the mixture into 1- to 2-inch oval patties. Roll in the bread crumbs.

Heat a heavy skillet over medium heat. Add 1 tablespoon oil and coat the pan.

Place 8 to 10 cutlets in a single layer. Pan-fry on medium heat for 7 to 10 minutes. Add 1 tablespoon oil tilting the pan to allow even coating. Turn cutlets over and fry the other side until golden brown. Repeat until all cutlets are done.

Serve immediately or reheat before serving. The cutlets can be served with ketchup or a variety of chutneys.

MAKES ABOUT
32 PAKORIES; 8 SERVINGS

PER SERVING

Calories 120

Carbohydrate 17 g

Fat 1.5 g

Saturated fat 0 g

Dietary fiber 1 g

Protein 9 g

Cholesterol 0 mg

Sodium 467 mg

EXCHANGES

1 starch

1 lean meat

MOONG BEAN BALLS WITH YOGURT

Dahi Pakori

This dish is served as a snack or a side dish. In northern India it is served with sweet and sour tamarind chutney as a chat (a type of dish that is typically spicy hot with some type of sweet and sour sauce). I like it hot and sour with lots of cayenne pepper and Tamarind Chutney (page 211). My friends from south India serve it without chutney, as a side dish. This is a mouth-watering healthy dish.

¾ cup moong dal (page 106)

⅓ cup cold water

2½ teaspoons salt

Vegetable oil for frying

2½ cups nonfat plain yogurt

½ cup skim milk

½ teaspoon Roasted Cumin Powder (page 49)

¼ to ½ teaspoon cayenne pepper

Clean the moong dal of any extraneous materials. Wash in 3 to 4 changes of water. Cover with water and soak overnight.

Drain the soaked dal in a strainer and rinse with cold water. Drain well. Place in a blender with the cold water and grind to a smooth paste. Continue to blend until the paste is light and fluffy. To test the batter, get a cup of cold water and with a fingertip drop a small amount of batter into the water. The batter should float to the top. If it does not float, blend a little longer and repeat the test. When the batter floats to the top, empty into a bowl and mix in ½ teaspoon of the salt. Set aside.

In a medium frying pan, heat 1 inch of oil over high heat. When the oil is very hot, add about 1 heaping teaspoon of batter at a time to the oil, using a teaspoon or your fingertips. Add as many balls as the pan will hold in a single layer. Fry on one side until light brown, turn over and fry the other side until light brown, about 5 minutes on each side. Drain with a slotted spoon and transfer to a paper towel–lined plate. Repeat with remaining batter. Set aside. (The pakories can be refrigerated or frozen for convenience. If frozen, thaw and use boiling hot water for soaking.) In a medium bowl of very hot water add 1 teaspoon of the salt and stir until dissolved. Add the pakories. Soak for 20 to 30 minutes.

In a medium bowl, lightly beat the yogurt, milk and remaining 1 teaspoon salt.

Remove the pakories from the soaking water by lightly squeezing 2 to 4 pakories between the palms of your hands. Take care not to break them. Add the squeezed pakories to the yogurt mixture. Discard the soaking water. Let stand at room temperature for 20 minutes or longer.

Before serving, garnish with the roasted cumin powder and cayenne pepper. Serve with Tamarind Chutney, if desired.

MAKES 6 SERVINGS

PER SERVING

Calories *147*

Carbohydrate *23 g*

Fat *3.6 g*

Saturated fat *0.5 g*

Dietary fiber *4.6 g*

Protein *5 g*

Cholesterol *0 mg*

Sodium *376 mg*

EXCHANGES

1½ starches

1 lean meat

STEAMED RICE AND BEAN CAKES
Dhokla

This is a very popular dish from the state of Gujarat. It is served as a snack or a side dish, usually with Coconut Chutney (page 213) or Tamarind Chutney (page 211). I like it with Sweet and Sour Cabbage (Sambhara, page 142) for lunch or as a light dinner.

½ cup chana dal (page 105)

½ cup long-grain rice

½ cup water

¼ cup plain nonfat yogurt

1 teaspoon salt

⅛ teaspoon turmeric

1 hot green chile, chopped (optional)

1 teaspoon chopped fresh ginger

½ teaspoon baking soda

1 tablespoon vegetable oil

Pinch of asafetida

½ teaspoon brown mustard seeds

6 to 8 curry leaves

1 tablespoon chopped cilantro

1 tablespoon grated fresh coconut (optional)

Clean the dal and rice of any extraneous materials. Wash in 3 to 4 changes of water. Cover with water and soak overnight.

Drain the dal and rice, discarding the water. Place the dal, rice, ½ cup water, yogurt, salt, turmeric, green chile, (if using) and ginger into a blender. Grind to a fine paste.

Place paste in a medium bowl and cover with a lid. Keep in a warm place for 12 to 24 hours. (I usually put it in the oven. To speed the process, I sometimes turn on the oven light for a few hours.) The dough will ferment and start to rise.

Bring 1 cup water to a boil in a Dutch oven or a large saucepan that is large enough to hold a 6- or 8-inch round or square metal cake pan. Brush or spray the cake pan with oil.

Add the baking soda to the fermented mixture and stir very gently from top to bottom, using a folding motion. Immediately transfer the mix to the cake pan, spreading evenly.

Using tongs, place the filled cake pan in the boiling water and cover with a lid. Reduce the heat and steam for 10 minutes. Remove from the heat and carefully take out the cake pan. Set aside to cool for 10 to 12 minutes. Cut the dhokla into 1-inch diamond shapes.

Heat the oil in a small frying pan over medium heat and add the asafetida and mustard seeds, covering with a lid to avoid splattering. Fry until the mustard seeds stop popping, a few seconds. Remove from the heat, add the curry leaves and cook for a few seconds. Evenly spread the oil mixture over the dhokla pieces.

Transfer to a serving platter and garnish with cilantro and grated coconut, if desired.

POUNDED RICE SNACK
Poha

MAKES 6
(⅔-CUP) SERVINGS

PER SERVING

Calories 178

Carbohydrate 29 g

Fat 5 g

Saturated fat 0.5 g

Dietary fiber 1.3 g

Protein 4 g

Cholesterol 0 mg

Sodium 370 mg

EXCHANGES

2 starches

1 fat

This quick, simple dish is often served for breakfast, a snack or a light meal. Poha is made of parboiled rice that is pounded or flattened and, therefore, takes just a few minutes to cook.

2 cups poha (pounded rice)

¼ teaspoon turmeric

1 teaspoon salt

4 teaspoons vegetable oil

½ teaspoon mustard seeds

6 to 8 curry leaves

1 tablespoon chana dal (page 105)

1 small onion, thinly sliced

½ cup frozen green peas

2 teaspoons coriander powder

½ teaspoon cayenne pepper (optional)

1 hot green chile, split lengthwise in half
   (optional)

⅓ cup water

1 tablespoon fresh lemon juice

2 tablespoons roasted Spanish peanuts
   (optional)

Clean the poha and wash in 1 to 2 changes of cold water. Drain in a strainer. Sprinkle with turmeric and salt and set aside.

Heat the oil in a nonstick frying pan over medium-high heat. Add the mustard seeds and cover with a lid to avoid splattering. Fry until the mustard seeds stop popping, a few seconds. Add the curry leaves and chana dal. Cook until the dal is light brown.

Add the onion and fry until light brown. Add the peas, coriander powder, cayenne pepper (if using) and green chile (if using). Stir, add the water and bring to a boil. Reduce the heat, cover and simmer for 7 to 8 minutes until the peas are done.

Add the poha and stir to mix well. Heat through and steam for about 2 minutes. Sprinkle with the lemon juice; stir. Garnish with the peanuts, if desired.

SNACK MIX
Chivra

MAKES 8
(½-CUP) SERVINGS

PER SERVING

Calories 110

Carbohydrate 11 g

Fat 7 g

Saturated fat 1 g

Dietary fiber 1 g

Protein 2 g

Cholesterol 0 mg

Sodium 191 mg

EXCHANGES

1 starch

1 fat

Hot spicy snacks are very popular in India. The variety is unlimited. Chivra is enjoyed as a snack anytime of the day and is usually spicy hot. Here is a quick and easy version using several available cereals.

1 ½ cups corn flakes

1 cup crisped rice cereal

1 cup puffed corn cereal

1 tablespoon vegetable oil

¼ teaspoon mustard seeds

½ cup mixed nuts

⅛ teaspoon cayenne pepper

¼ teaspoon salt

¼ teaspoon black pepper

¼ teaspoon mango powder

Combine the cereals and set aside.

Heat the oil in a large skillet over medium heat. Add the mustard seeds to the hot oil and cover with a lid to avoid splattering. Fry until the mustard seeds stop popping, a few seconds. Reduce heat to low. Add the cereal mix and stir well. Add the nuts, cayenne pepper, salt, black pepper and mango powder. Roast, stirring occasionally for 5 to 7 minutes. Remove from the heat and cool completely.

Store in an airtight container.

CREAM OF WHEAT SNACK
Uppama

MAKES 8
(½-CUP) SERVINGS

PER SERVING
Calories 115
Carbohydrate 19 g
Fat 2.7 g
Saturated fat 0.3 g
Dietary fiber 2.3 g
Protein 3 g
Cholesterol 0 mg
Sodium 281 mg

EXCHANGES
1 starch
1 vegetable
½ fat

Uppama is served most commonly at breakfast, although it may be served as a snack or a light meal. This is a very popular dish in south India. We enjoy it for lunch, so I usually put vegetables in it. It may also be made plain with just spices and/or onions.

1 cup cream of wheat

4 teaspoons vegetable oil

½ teaspoon mustard seeds

6 to 8 curry leaves

1 tablespoon chana dal (page 105)

1 small onion, thinly sliced

½ cup frozen green peas

½ cup diced carrot

½ teaspoon cayenne pepper (optional)

1 teaspoon salt

3½ cups water

Dry-roast the cream of wheat in a heavy skillet over medium heat, stirring constantly, until the cream of wheat turns light brown, 7 to 10 minutes. Transfer to a plate and set aside.

Heat the oil in the same skillet over medium-high heat. Add the mustard seeds, cover with a lid and fry until the mustard seeds stop popping, a few seconds. Add the curry leaves and chana dal; cook until the dal is light brown, stirring occasionally.

Add the onion and fry until light brown. Add the peas, carrots, cayenne pepper (if using) and salt. Stir and fry for a few seconds. Add the water and bring to a boil.

Gradually add the roasted cream of wheat with one hand as you stir with the other. Keep stirring, breaking up any lumps until the cream of wheat is well mixed with the water. Cover with a lid, reduce the heat and simmer until most of the water is absorbed, 10 to 12 minutes.

Let stand until ready to serve. Stir before serving.

POTATO-STUFFED PASTRIES
Samosas

Samosas are one of the most popular snacks of India, and potato-stuffed samosas are the most common, although they can be filled with lamb or something sweet. Hot samosas served with tea make any afternoon a delight. Serve them with Cilantro Chutney (page 209), Tamarind Chutney (page 211) or ketchup.

FILLING
5 medium potatoes

2 teaspoons vegetable oil

½ teaspoon cumin seeds

1 tablespoon chopped fresh ginger

¾ cup frozen green peas

2 teaspoons salt

1 tablespoon coriander powder

1 hot green chile, chopped (optional)

1 teaspoon mango powder

1 tablespoon Garam Masala (page 48) or purchased

¼ cup water

DOUGH
2 cups all-purpose flour

½ teaspoon salt

3 tablespoons vegetable oil

½ cup water

ASSEMBLY
¼ cup water

Vegetable oil, for frying

To prepare the filling: Cook the potatoes in boiling water until tender. To prevent the potatoes from getting sticky, remove from the boiling water as soon as they are done and cool completely.

Peel and mash the potatoes into about ½-inch pieces, not necessarily of uniform size.

In a large frying pan, heat the oil over medium-high heat. When the oil is hot, add the cumin seeds. Fry until the cumin seeds are golden brown, a few seconds. Add the ginger and stir. Stir in the potatoes and peas.

Add the salt, coriander powder, green chile (if using), mango powder and Garam Masala. Mix thoroughly. Stir in the water. Cover with a lid, reduce heat to medium-low and cook for 2 to 3 minutes. Stir and let stand, cover for 5 to 7 minutes. Remove the lid and cool.

To prepare the dough: In a bowl, mix the flour, salt and oil. Add water gradually as you mix. (This can be done in a food processor or dough maker.)

Turn the dough out onto a floured surface and knead for 5 minutes or until the dough becomes smooth and soft. Divide the dough into 10 balls.

To assemble the samosas: Roll each ball into a 5- to 6-inch circle. Cut each in half. Put the ¼ cup water in a small bowl; set aside. Take one half circle, dip your finger in the water and run it along the straight edge. Fold in half, joining the straight edges, making a cone. Seal edges tightly. Fill with 2 tablespoons of filling. Dip your finger in the water and run along the inside of the open side and seal tightly. Keep the filled samosas between towels to avoid drying.

Heat the oil in a wok or frying pan over medium-high until hot enough that when you drop a pinch of dough into the oil the dough floats up within seconds. (It is important to have the oil the right temperature. If the oil is too hot, the samosas will not cook inside; if the oil is not hot enough, the samosas might fall apart in the oil or get greasy.) Fry 3 to 5 samosas at a time until light golden brown, 4 to 5 minutes on each side.

Serve hot with chutney or ketchup. They can be reheated in the oven.

QUICK SAMOSAS

MAKES 20 SAMOSAS

PER SAMOSA

Calories 114

Carbohydrate 16 g

Fat 5 g

Saturated fat 0.6 g

Dietary fiber 1 g

Protein 2 g

Cholesterol 0 mg

Sodium 220 mg

EXCHANGES

1 starch

1 fat

I love samosas but making them can be quite a task. I make my samosas with a flour tortilla for the shell. They taste great and take only a quarter of the time and effort. The fresher the tortillas, the easier it is to work with them.

2 tablespoons all-purpose flour

4 tablespoons water

10 small flour tortillas

In a small bowl mix the flour and water to make a paste; set aside.

Heat a frying pan over low heat. Cut one tortilla in half. Warm one half in the frying pan for a few seconds. When it is soft, remove from the pan. Immediately make into a cone using the flour paste to seal the edges. Follow the directions on pages 72–73 for filling and frying samosas.

INDIAN BREADS

Wheat is the main staple food for north Indians. A variety of wheat breads are eaten at most meals. The most common bread is *roti*, which may also be called *phulka* or *chapati*. Roti is the correct Indian name, *chapati* is a word created by the British. It is an unleavened bread made of whole wheat flour. The whole wheat flour available in India is made of a different variety of wheat that grinds up finer than the wheat flour available in the United States. Most stores that carry Indian groceries carry durum wheat flour or *roti/chapati* flour, which comes from Canada. This flour makes softer Indian breads. If you are unable to get durum wheat flour, you can combine whole wheat flour with all-purpose flour to make the *roties* in the recipes.

The most common *roti* is made on a *tava* or iron griddle. It is a thin and flat bread, similar in appearance to a tortilla but very different in taste. For north Indians nothing is more satisfying and filling than a hot *roti* served with a meal. The varieties of breads include *paratha*—plain or stuffed (pan-fried)—*puri* (deep-fried) and *kachori* (stuffed *puri*).

Naan is a leavened flat bread made of white flour and is commonly served in restaurants. It is made in a clay oven, or *tandoor*, which gives this bread a very special taste.

Making *roties* is time-consuming and requires practice and skill. I have found that baking *roties* in the oven does not require the same skill or practice as making *roties* on a griddle. I broil the *roties* and *naan*. Not every one can have a *tandoor* in the house or go to the restaurant everyday, but everyone can enjoy the goodness of *roti* or *naan* at home. The taste of a warm *roti* is irresistible. Try these very simple, quick, low-fat versions of Indian breads.

If durum wheat flour is not available, substitute ¾ cup whole wheat flour and ¼ cup all-purpose flour for 1 cup of durum wheat flour. The amount of water needed to make the same consistency of dough for the two types of flours varies, so add water carefully.

For the nutritional analyses, I used three parts whole wheat flour and one part all-purpose flour.

MAKES 8 ROTIES

PER ROTI

Calories 100

Carbohydrate 22 g

Fat 0 g

Saturated fat 0 g

Dietary fiber 3 g

Protein 4 g

Cholesterol 0 mg

Sodium 0 mg

EXCHANGES

1½ starches

OVEN ROTI

Tandoori Roti

Tandoori roti is supposed to be made in a tandoor (clay oven), but I make it in a conventional oven. This is a very easy and fast way to have roties, because you can make several at a time. Because they are thicker than the everyday roties, you may only have to make half as many.

> **Roti dough (page 78)**
> **½ cup all-purpose flour, for rolling**
> **2 tablespoons ghee or butter (optional)**

Preheat the broiler. Place the flour for rolling in a shallow container.

Make the dough according to the directions. Divide the dough into 8 balls. Roll each ball between the palms of your hands in a circular motion until the dough is smooth. Press to flatten. Coat each piece in the flour. Then roll each into an oval or round about ¼ inch thick.

Place 3 to 4 roties on a lightly greased baking sheet. Broil in the middle of the oven for 2 to 3 minutes, until puffed and light brown. Turn over and broil for 1 to 2 minutes until slightly brown on the other side.

Serve immediately or place in an airtight container to serve later. Brush roti on the first side with ghee or butter, if desired.

PER ROTI

Calories 80

Carbohydrate 16 g

Fat 0 g

Saturated fat 0 g

Dietary fiber 2 g

Protein 3 g

Cholesterol 0 mg

Sodium 0 mg

EXCHANGES

1 starch

ROTI
Phulka

Roti, phulka or chapati are all different names for the flat breads made of whole wheat flour. Phulka is typically a thin puffed roti. This is the most common type of roti made fresh at every meal. Thin roties may look like tortillas but taste quite different. They are made on a tava (flat iron griddle) on the stovetop. If you do not have a tava use a heavy fry pan.

> **2 cups durum wheat flour or 1½ cups whole wheat flour and ½ cup all-purpose flour**
>
> **⅞ to 1 cup water**
>
> **½ cup all-purpose flour, for rolling**
>
> **2 tablespoons ghee or butter (optional)**

In a mixing bowl combine the flours. (The dough can also be made in a food processor or dough maker.) Make a hole in the center of the flour. Add the water gradually as you mix the dough. (Depending on the type of flour, the amount of water needed may vary slightly.) The dough should be soft and easy to roll into a ball. Knead the dough thoroughly until smooth and elastic. The dough should resemble a yeast bread dough in consistency and smoothness. Cover and let sit for 10 minutes or longer.

Heat a tava (cast iron flat griddle) or a heavy frying pan over medium heat. Place ½ cup flour for rolling in a shallow container.

Divide the dough into 12 balls. Roll each ball between the palms of your hands in a circular motion until the dough is smooth. Press to flatten. Coat each piece in the flour. Then using the flour as needed, roll each piece into a circle about 6 inches in diameter.

Place the roti on the heated tava or frying pan. Cook until it turns color and becomes firm and easy to pick up, 10 to 20 seconds. Turn it over and cook on the other side until light brown, 15 to 20 seconds. Turn it back to the first side and, using a folded kitchen towel, press the roti down gently but firmly. The roti will puff as you press it.

Brush the roti on the first side with ghee or butter, if desired. The ghee or butter keeps the roties soft and moist. Serve immediately or place in an air-tight container to serve later.

POTATO-STUFFED ROTI
Tandoori Alu Roti

MAKES 12 ROTIES

PER ROTI

Calories 115

Carbohydrate 21 g

Fat 2 g

Saturated fat 1 g

Dietary fiber 2.4 g

Protein 3 g

Cholesterol 5 mg

Sodium 199 mg

EXCHANGES

1½ starches

This is a quick and low-fat version of potato paratha (pan-fried roti), a stuffed fried roti very popular in Northern India. They are relatively high in fat. I make these roties for breakfast or as a simple meal. Serve them with plain yogurt, Indian pickles and salad. Serve them with your favorite meal instead of your usual bread.

DOUGH

2 cups durum wheat flour or 1½ cups whole wheat flour and ½ cup all-purpose flour

½ teaspoon salt

⅞ to 1 cup water

FILLING

3 medium whole potatoes, boiled

½ teaspoon salt

1 teaspoon coriander powder

½ teaspoon cayenne pepper (optional)

1 hot green chile, finely chopped (optional)

ASSEMBLY

½ cup all-purpose flour for rolling

2 tablespoons ghee or butter

To make the dough: In a bowl, combine the flours and salt. (The dough can be made in a food processor or dough maker.) Make a hole in the center of the flour. Add the water gradually as you mix the dough. (Depending on the type of flour, the amount of water needed may vary slightly.) The dough should be soft but easy to roll into a ball. Knead the dough thoroughly until smooth and elastic. The dough should resemble yeast bread dough in consistency and smoothness. Cover and let stand for 10 minutes or longer.

To make the filling: Peel the potatoes and mash in a plate. The potatoes should be in about ¼-inch pieces or smaller. Add the salt and coriander powder, cayenne pepper (if using) and green chile (if using). Mix well. Divide filling into 12 equal portions.

To assemble the roties: Preheat the broiler. Place the flour for rolling in a shallow container.

Divide the dough into 12 balls. Roll each ball between the palms of your hands in a circular motion until the dough is smooth. Press to flatten. Coat each piece in the flour. Roll out each into a circle about 3 inches in diameter. Place one portion of the filling in the center of each. Now lift the edges of each circle, keeping the filling in the center, and join the edges in the center. Crimp the edges tightly and flatten with the palm of your hand. Pick up the filled ball and roll again in the flour. Place each one filled side down and roll to a ¼-inch-thick oval or round.

Place 3 to 4 roties on a lightly greased baking sheet. Broil in the middle of the oven for 2 to 3 minutes, until light brown. Turn over and broil for 1 to 2 minutes, until light brown on the other side.

Brush the roti on the first side with ghee or butter. Serve immediately or place in an airtight container to serve later.

CHICKPEA-FLOUR ROTI

Missi Roti

MAKES 8 ROTIES

PER ROTI

Calories 204

Carbohydrate 34 g

Fat 4 g

Saturated fat 1.8 g

Dietary fiber 8.2 g

Protein 8 g

Cholesterol 8 mg

Sodium 311 mg

EXCHANGES

2 starches

1 fat

I grew up eating this roti for breakfast on Sunday mornings when the whole family was at home. It is very filling and tastes great. Of course it was extra rich, because Mom served it with a scoop of fresh creamy butter. But now I eat it with just a small amount of butter to reduce the amount of fat.

2 cups durum wheat flour or 1½ cups whole wheat flour and ½ cup all-purpose flour

1½ cups chickpea flour (besan)

1 medium onion, finely chopped

1 teaspoon salt

1⅛ cups water

½ cup durham wheat flour, for rolling

2 tablespoons butter

In a bowl, combine the wheat flour, chickpea flour, onion and salt; mix well. Add the water gradually as you make the dough. The dough should be soft but easy to roll into a ball. Cover and set aside for 15 minutes. (This dough cannot be made in a food processor or dough maker because it tends to get sticky.)

Heat a tava (cast-iron flat griddle) or a heavy frying pan over medium heat. Place the flour for rolling in a shallow container.

Oil your hands lightly and knead the dough to make it smooth. Divide the dough into 8 balls. Roll each ball between the palms of your hands until it is a smooth, flattened ball. Coat the balls in the flour. Then using the flour as needed, roll each into a round about ¼ inch thick.

Place the roti on the heated tava or frying pan. Cook until the roti turns color or becomes firm and is easy to pick up, about 1 minute. Turn it over and cook on the other side until light brown on the second side, about 1 minute. Remove and set aside. Continue cooking all the roties in the same fashion.

Preheat the broiler. Place the roties on a lightly greased baking sheet. Broil in the middle of the oven for 2 to 3 minutes, until golden brown. Turn over and broil for 1 to 2 minutes more until light brown.

Brush each roti on the first side with ½ teaspoon butter. Serve immediately. This roti does not keep well. If you need to cook them in advance, cook on the tava and then broil just before serving.

MAKES 8 ROTIES

PER ROTI
Calories 128
Carbohydrate 22 g
Fat 3 g
Saturated fat 1.8 g
Dietary fiber 3 g
Protein 4 g
Cholesterol 8 mg
Sodium 1 mg

EXCHANGES
1½ starches
½ fat

COILED ROTI
Ghee Ke Hath Ki Roti

We all love this roti—it is crispy and has a very wheaty warm flavor. The name ghee ke hath ki roti (roti made with ghee hands) may make you think it is high in fat, but it is not; it just uses ghee for rolling instead of flour. Cook this roti until golden brown and crispy. Serve it with Kidney Beans (Rajmah, page 114) or Whole Urad Dal (Dal Makhani, page 112). You can also use margarine, if desired.

Roti dough (page 78)
2 tablespoons ghee or butter

Make the dough according to directions.

Heat a tava (cast-iron flat griddle) or a heavy frying pan over medium heat. Divide the dough into 8 balls. Roll each ball between the palms of your hands until it is a smooth, flattened ball. Lightly grease a clean surface and rolling pin. Roll each ball into a round about a ¼ inch thick. Put ½ teaspoon ghee on the surface of each round and spread it with your finger. With your fingers, lift one side of the round and roll toward you, making a tight roll, like a rope. Now take this roll and make a circle in a coiled shape. Pick it up in your palms, flatten just a little bit and press to make it stick together in a flat circle. Roll again into a ¼-inch-thick round, using a dab of ghee to prevent sticking, if necessary.

Place 1 roti on the heated tava or frying pan. Cook until it becomes firm and is easy to pick up, about 1 minute. Turn the roti over and cook it on the other side until light brown, about 1 minute. Remove and set aside.

Preheat the broiler. Place the roties on a lightly greased baking sheet. Broil in the middle of the oven for 2 to 3 minutes, until golden brown. Turn over and broil for 1 to 2 minutes more, until light brown.

Brush each roti on the first side with ½ teaspoon ghee. Serve immediately. This roti does not keep well. If you need to cook them in advance, cook on the tava and then broil just before serving.

MAKES 12 NAANS

PER NAAN
Calories 124
Carbohydrate 24 g
Fat 1 g
Saturated fat 0 g
Dietary fiber 0.5 g
Protein 4 g
Cholesterol 0 mg
Sodium 11 mg

EXCHANGES
1½ starches

TANDOORI BREAD

Naan

Naan originally came from the Middle East. It is a very popular bread served in Indian restaurants. It is supposed to be made in a tandoor (clay oven), but here is a way to make naan in your very own oven.

3 cups all-purpose flour

¾ cup nonfat plain yogurt

½ teaspoon active dry yeast

1 teaspoon sugar

½ cup lukewarm water

1 tablespoon vegetable oil

In a food processor or dough maker, combine the flour and yogurt. (The dough can also be made by hand in a mixing bowl.)

Dissolve the yeast and sugar in the lukewarm water. Add to the flour and process until the dough is smooth. The dough should resemble yeast bread dough in consistency and smoothness.

Transfer the dough to a bowl, coat it evenly with oil and knead a few times. Cover with a lid and let the dough rise for 3 to 4 hours. Divide the dough into 12 equal portions. Roll each portion between the palms of your hands to make a smooth ball.

Preheat the broiler. Using a lightly oiled surface and rolling pin, roll out each ball to an oval about ¼ inch thick.

Place 3 to 4 naans on a lightly greased baking sheet. Broil in the middle of the oven for 2 to 3 minutes, until they slightly puff and are lightly browned. Turn over and broil for 1 to 2 minutes. (Do not overcook the naans, because they will become dry.) Serve immediately or cool and store in an airtight container.

PER NAAN

Calories *133*

Carbohydrate *20 g*

Fat *3 g*

Saturated fat *1 g*

Dietary fiber *0.6 g*

Protein *6 g*

Cholesterol *8 mg*

Sodium *111 mg*

EXCHANGES

1 starch

1 lean meat

CHEESE-STUFFED NAAN

Paneer Ke Naan

Ricotta cheese or paneer can be used to make this very special recipe. Stuffed naans are a specialty, the spiced cheese adds a wonderful taste. My children love these. They make a great accompaniment to any meal.

> **Naan dough (page 85)**
>
> **1 ½ cups reduced-fat ricotta cheese or Paneer (page 52)**
>
> **½ teaspoon salt**
>
> **1 teaspoon coriander powder**
>
> **½ teaspoon cayenne pepper (optional)**

Prepare the naan dough; let it rise as directed

In a heavy nonstick frying pan, cook the ricotta cheese or paneer over medium heat, stirring occasionally. Cook until all the water is evaporated and the cheese is slightly crumbly. Transfer to a plate and cool completely. Add the salt, coriander powder and cayenne pepper (if using) to the cheese and mix well.

Divide the dough into 15 pieces. Roll each between the palms of your hands to make a smooth ball.

Using a lightly oiled surface and rolling pin, roll out each ball to a circle about 3 inches in diameter and place cheese mixture in the center of each circle. Lift the edges of the circle, bring to the center, slightly overlapping, and crimp the edges together. Press with the palm of your hand onto the rolling surface. Turn the stuffed ball over placing the filled side down. Cover and let sit for 5 to 10 minutes.

Preheat the broiler. Roll out each ball into an oval or circle ¼ inch thick, using oil if necessary.

Place the naans on a lightly greased baking sheet. Broil in the middle of oven for 2 to 3 minutes, until they are lightly browned. Turn over and broil for 1 to 2 minutes more, until light brown. Serve immediately or store in an airtight container.

RICE

Rice is the staple grain in south and east India. It is the most versatile grain available. Rice can be cooked plain or with meat, vegetables and a variety of spices. In India, mostly plain rice is eaten. Plain rice goes well with *dal*, meat, vegetables or yogurt.

Long-grain and basmati rice are the most common kinds of rice eaten in India. Basmati rice is an extra-long-grain rice with a naturally mild aroma. The basmati rice is a little more expensive and often eaten on special occasions or for special rice dishes like *pulao* or *biriyani*. When cooked, basmati rice is long, slender and fluffy. Long-grain rice is a little more sticky and has a very good taste. Parboiled or other packaged rice is generally not used in Indian meals. Rice is easy to cook if you keep a few steps in mind. In my cooking classes, people often mention how difficult it is to cook fluffy rice.

Here are some general rules for cooking perfect rice.

1. Use a pan large enough for the rice to expand. My general rule of thumb is a one quart-sized pan for every cup of rice, for example, one quart for one cup, or two quarts for two cups. You can use a larger pan, but if you use a smaller one you will have sticky rice or unevenly cooked rice, because the grains will get packed and not have room to expand. Make sure the pan has a tightly fitted lid.

2. If you buy packaged long-grain rice you do not have to clean it. If you buy basmati rice, you might have to clean it of any extraneous materials like small rocks or unhulled rice. Always wash rice in three to four changes of cold water. Washing gets rid of any starchy powder and makes the rice less sticky.

To wash rice, place it in a bowl and add cold water. I usually stir with my hand as I lightly rub the rice. Use your hands to keep the rice in the bowl as you drain the water. Repeat the process until the water is relatively clear.

3. Soak the rice in cold water for about thirty minutes. Soaking rice makes the rice grains longer and reduces the stickiness.

4. Drain the rice and discard the water.

5. Add 2 cups of water for 1 cup of rice. For each additional cup of rice, reduce the water by ⅛ cup; for example, for 2 cups of rice use 3⅞ cups of water, for 3 cups of rice use 5¾ cups of water.

6. Bring the rice to a full boil, reduce the heat and simmer, uncovered, for about seven minutes. Partially cover with lid and continue to simmer undisturbed for another seven to eight minutes. Check if the rice is done by placing one or two grains of rice on the countertop and gently pressing with a finger. If the rice is not done, you will feel the grain under your finger; add a little more water and continue to cook. If the rice is done, remove it from the heat, cover with a lid and let stand until ready to serve.

7. Before serving, gently fluff rice with a fork or a butter knife. Lift the rice and gently break up any lumps.

8. To reheat rice, steam with one to two tablespoons of water or for the best results, reheat in a microwave oven until steamy hot.

PLAIN RICE

Basmati Chawal

MAKES 10
(⅓-CUP) SERVINGS

PER SERVING

Calories 68

Carbohydrate 16 g

Fat 0 g

Saturated fat 0 g

Dietary fiber 0.2 g

Protein 1 g

Cholesterol 0 mg

Sodium 0 mg

EXCHANGE

1 starch

Basmati rice is a variety of rice that is extra long and has a very nice aroma. When cooked it is fluffy and light. Some people eat basmati rice everyday and some people use it only for special occasions or special rice dishes. It cooks just like other long-grain rice.

> 1 cup basmati rice
>
> 2 cups water

Clean the rice, removing any unhulled rice or other extraneous material. Wash in 2 to 3 changes of water until the washing water is relatively clear. Soak in cold water for ½ hour or longer. (Soaking helps make the rice grains longer. If you don't have time, this soaking can be eliminated.) Drain the rice in a strainer.

Add the rice and 2 cups water to a 2-quart or larger saucepan. Bring the water to a boil. Reduce the heat to a simmer. Cover with a lid, leaving it ajar for the steam to escape. Simmer until the water is absorbed for 10 to 15 minutes. Check if the rice is done by placing 1 or 2 grains of rice on the countertop and gently pressing with your finger. If the rice is not done, you will feel the grain under your finger; add a little more water and continue to cook.

Remove the pan from the heat. Cover with a lid until ready to serve. Before serving, stir gently from the bottom with a fork as you fluff the rice.

MAKES 15
(⅓-CUP) SERVINGS

PER SERVING

Calories 73

Carbohydrate 15 g

Fat 0.5 g

Saturated fat 0 g

Dietary fiber 0.2 g

Protein 1 g

Cholesterol 0 mg

Sodium 143 mg

EXCHANGE

1 starch

ROASTED RICE

Bhuna Chawal

This rice tastes and smells great. The whole spices add a wonderful flavor to the rice. Yet the flavor is not overpowering and is an excellent accompaniment to any dinner party dish. The whole spices, by the way, are not eaten.

1 ½ cups basmati rice

¼ teaspoon cumin seeds

6 to 8 black peppercorns

½-inch cinnamon stick

2 whole cloves

1 whole cardamom, crushed

2 bay leaves

2 teaspoons vegetable oil

3 cups water

1 teaspoon salt

Clean the rice, removing any unhulled rice or other extraneous material. Wash in 2 to 3 changes of water until the water is relatively clear. Soak in cold water for ½ hour or longer. (Soaking can be eliminated to save time.) Drain the rice in a strainer; set aside.

Combine the cumin seeds, peppercorns, cinnamon stick, cloves, cardamom and bay leaves in a small bowl; set aside.

Heat the oil in a 2- to 3-quart saucepan over medium-high heat. Add the spices and fry until the cumin seeds are golden brown, a few seconds. (All the spices will puff.) Add the rice and fry for 2 to 3 minutes, stirring constantly. Take care not to break the rice.

Add the water and salt. Bring to a boil and reduce the heat to a simmer. Partially cover with a lid, leaving the lid ajar for steam to escape. Simmer 15 to 20 minutes. Check if the rice is done by placing 1 or 2 grains of rice on the countertop and gently pressing with your finger. If the rice is not done you will feel the grain under your finger; add a little more water and continue to cook.

Remove from the heat. Cover with a lid until ready to serve. Before serving, fluff the rice with a fork by gently stirring from the bottom.

RICE PILAF WITH PEAS

Matar Pulao

PER SERVING

Calories 169

Carbohydrate 30 g

Fat 3.5 g

Saturated fat 0.5 g

Dietary fiber 1 g

Protein 3 g

Cholesterol 0 mg

Sodium 281 mg

EXCHANGES

2 starches

½ fat

This is a great addition to a special meal. In my house it was often served with corian-der chutney and plain yogurt as a quick and light Sunday lunch. This low-fat version has all the flavor of the traditional pilaf with a fraction of the fat. Do not eat the whole spices.

1 ½ cups basmati rice

½ teaspoon cumin seeds

½-inch stick cinnamon

2 whole cloves

2 cardamom pods

2 bay leaves

1 tablespoon vegetable oil

1 small onion, thinly sliced

¾ cup frozen green peas

1 ½ teaspoons Garam Masala (page 48) or purchased

2¾ cups water

1 teaspoon salt

Clean the rice, removing any unhulled rice or other extraneous material. Wash in 2 to 3 changes of water until the washing water is relatively clear. Soak in cold water for ½ hour or longer. (Soaking can be eliminated to save time.) Drain the rice in a strainer; set aside.

Combine the cumin seeds, cinnamon stick, cloves, cardamom and bay leaves in a small bowl; set aside.

Heat the oil in a 3- to 4-quart saucepan over medium-high heat. Add the spices and fry until the cumin seeds are golden brown, a few seconds. (All the spices will puff.) Add the onion and fry until it is golden brown, stirring occasionally. Add the drained rice and fry for 2 to 3 minutes longer, stirring constantly. Take care not to break the rice.

Add the peas, garam masala, water and salt. Stir gently to mix.

Bring to a boil and reduce the heat to a simmer. Partially cover with a lid, leaving the lid ajar for the steam to escape. Simmer until the water is absorbed, for 15 to 20 minutes, gently stirring once or twice. Check if the rice is done by placing 1 or 2 grains of rice on the countertop and gently pressing with your finger. If the rice is not done, you will feel the grain under your finger; add a little more water and continue to cook.

Remove from the heat. Cover with a lid until ready to serve. Before serving, gently stir and fluff rice with a fork by gently stirring from the bottom.

VEGETABLE RICE

Tahari

MAKES 8
(½-CUP) SERVINGS

PER SERVING

Calories 100

Carbohydrate 21 g

Fat 0.5 g

Saturated fat 0 g

Dietary fiber 0.7 g

Protein 2 g

EXCHANGES

1½ starches

Tahari can be made with the vegetables of your choice. It is often made with cauliflower and potatoes or peas. I use mixed vegetables for convenience and variety. Serve with plain yogurt and Cilantro Chutney (page 209) or pickles for a light, quick meal.

1 cup long-grain or basmati rice

2½ cups water

1 teaspoon salt

1 teaspoon vegetable oil

½ teaspoon cumin seeds

1 cup frozen mixed vegetables

¼ teaspoon turmeric

¼ teaspoon Garam Masala (page 48) or purchased

1 teaspoon fresh lemon juice

Clean the rice, removing any unhulled rice or other extraneous material. Wash in 2 to 3 changes of water until the washing water is relatively clear. Soak in cold water for ½ hour or longer. (Soaking helps make the rice grains longer. If you don't have time, this soaking can be eliminated). Drain the rice in a strainer.

Add the rice, 2 cups of the water and ¾ teaspoon of the salt to a 2-quart saucepan. Bring the water to a boil. Reduce the heat to a simmer. Cover with a lid, leaving the lid ajar for the steam to escape. Simmer until the water is absorbed, 10 to 15 minutes. Check if the rice is done by placing 1 or 2 grains of rice on the countertop and gently pressing with your finger. If the rice is not done you will feel the grain under your finger; add a little more water and continue to cook.

In the meantime, heat the oil in a heavy 2- to 3-quart saucepan over medium heat. Add the cumin seeds and fry until they are golden brown, a few seconds. Add the mixed vegetables, the remaining ¼ teaspoon salt, the turmeric and the remaining ½ cup water. Bring to a boil, cover with a lid, reduce heat and simmer for 10 minutes. Add the garam masala and stir to combine.

Add the rice to the vegetables, mixing gently to avoid breaking rice. Sprinkle with the lemon juice and stir to combine. Cover and let sit until ready to serve.

VEGETABLE-RICE CASSEROLE

Subji Biriyani

MAKES 6
(1-CUP) SERVINGS

PER SERVING

Calories 310

Carbohydrate 45 g

Fat 10 g

Saturated fat 1.5 g

Dietary fiber 3 g

Protein 9 g

Cholesterol 0 mg

Sodium 573 mg

EXCHANGES

3 starches

2 fats

Biriyani is most commonly made with lamb or chicken. This one has all the goodness of vegetables and beans and tastes great—a meal in itself.

1 cup basmati rice

½ cup moong dal (page 106)

5 cups water

¼ teaspoon turmeric

1 ½ teaspoons salt

¼ cup unsalted dry roasted peanuts

1 small onion, coarsely chopped

½ teaspoon cumin seeds

1 teaspoon cayenne pepper (optional)

2 tablespoons vegetable oil

1 small potato, peeled and chopped into ¼-inch cubes

1 medium carrot, peeled and chopped into ¼-inch cubes

1 small tomato, chopped into ½-inch cubes

½ cup frozen green peas

¼ cup cashews, chopped

¼ cup golden raisins

½ cup plain nonfat yogurt

Clean the rice and moong dal of any extraneous material. Combine them and wash in 2 to 3 changes of water until the washing water is relatively clear. Strain and set aside.

In a 2 to 3 quart saucepan, add the rice and dal mixture, 3 cups of the water, the turmeric and 1 teaspoon of the salt. Bring to a boil. Reduce the heat to a simmer. Cover with a lid, leaving it ajar for steam to escape. Simmer until all the water is absorbed and the rice is soft, 12 to 15 minutes.

In the meantime, coarsely grind the peanuts in a blender and set aside.

To make the onion masala, in the same blender, finely grind the onion, cumin seeds and cayenne pepper (if using). (You may need to add 1 to 2 tablespoons water to be able to grind.) Set aside. Heat a heavy nonstick 4-quart skillet over medium heat. Add the onion mixture. Cook until most of the water is evaporated, a few seconds. Add the oil and fry until the onion masala is light brown.

Add the ground peanuts, potato, carrot, tomato, peas, cashews, raisins and remaining ½ teaspoon salt. Mix well. Add 1 cup of the remaining water, bring to a boil and reduce the heat. Cover with a lid and simmer until vegetables are tender, 8 to 10 minutes, stirring occasionally.

Beat the yogurt lightly and add, 1 tablespoon at a time, to the vegetables, stirring constantly. Cook for 5 to 7 minutes, uncovered, stirring occasionally to blend the yogurt with the vegetables.

Add the remaining 1 cup water and bring to a boil. Add the cooked rice and dal mixture. Stir gently with a spatula to avoid breaking rice. Cover with a lid and steam through for 2 to 3 minutes.

Remove from the heat, cover and let stand until ready to serve. Fluff with a fork before serving.

SWEET RICE

Meethe Chawal

MAKES 12
(⅓-CUP) SERVINGS

PER SERVING

Calories 123

Carbohydrate 29 g

Fat 0.5 g

Saturated fat 0 g

Dietary fiber 0.3 g

Protein 1 g

Cholesterol 0 mg

Sodium 0 mg

EXCHANGES

2 starches

Sweet rice is usually served at the end of a meal. It is very popular in north India. In Rajasthan it is often made when company comes or for a special occasion, and there it is served with the meal. Here is an easy, low-fat and foolproof method of making this dish. Enjoy it as a side dish or a dessert. It is best when served warm.

> 1 cup basmati rice
>
> 2 cups water
>
> ¼ teaspoon saffron threads
>
> ½-inch cinnamon stick
>
> 1 cup sugar
>
> 2 tablespoons blanched slivered almonds

Clean the rice, removing any unhulled rice or other extraneous material. Wash in 2 to 3 changes of water until the washing water is relatively clear. Soak in cold water for ½ hour or longer. (Soaking helps make the rice grains longer. If you don't have time, this soaking can be eliminated.) Drain the rice in a strainer.

To a 2-quart saucepan, add the 2 cups water, saffron threads and cinnamon stick. Bring the water to a boil, add the rice and bring to a boil again. Reduce the heat to a simmer. Cover with a lid, leaving it ajar for the steam to escape. Simmer 15 to 20 minutes. Check if the rice is done by placing 1 or 2 grains of rice on the countertop and gently pressing with your finger. If the rice is not done, you will feel the grain under your finger; add a little more water and continue to cook.

Add the sugar, cover with a lid and cook for 1 to 2 minutes. Remove from the heat and let sit for 10 to 15 minutes. Remove the lid and mix gently with a fork. Cover and let sit for 10 minutes or until ready to serve.

Before serving, fluff rice with a fork by stirring gently from the bottom. Garnish with the almonds.

PER SERVING

Calories 77

Carbohydrate 15 g

Fat 1 g

Saturated fat 0 g

Dietary fiber 0.2 g

Protein 1 g

Cholesterol 0 mg

Sodium 214 mg

EXCHANGE

1 starch

LEMON RICE
Neembu Chawal

This is a very popular dish in south India. The spices and lemon juice turn plain rice into an exotic dish. It is great for leftover rice. Serve it as a side dish with any meal.

1 cup long grain rice, cooked (page 87)

1 tablespoon vegetable oil

½ teaspoon brown mustard seeds

6 to 8 curry leaves

1 tablespoon chana dal (page 105)

⅛ teaspoon turmeric

½ teaspoon cayenne pepper (optional)

2 tablespoons fresh lemon juice

1 teaspoon salt

Cool the rice slightly. Heat the oil in a heavy skillet over medium-high heat. Add the mustard seeds and cover with a lid to avoid splattering. Fry until the mustard seeds stop popping, a few seconds. Add the curry leaves and chana dal. Cook until the dal is light brown, a few seconds. Remove from the heat. Stir in the turmeric and cayenne pepper (if using). Let stand a few seconds; add the lemon juice.

Add the rice and salt, mixing gently to avoid breaking the rice. Return to the heat and cook until hot. Serve cold or warm.

STEAMED RICE DUMPLINGS
Idli

Idlies are originally from south India, but now they have become very popular all over India. This is an easy recipe and the idlies comes out very light and fluffy. Use idli containers or cake pans to steam idli. Serve them warm with Toor Dal with Vegetables (Sambhar, page 122), and Coconut Chutney (page 213).

> ½ cup urad dal (page 106)
>
> 1 cup water
>
> 1¼ cups cream of rice
>
> 1 teaspoon salt

Clean the dal of any extraneous materials and soak for 2 hours or longer.

Wash the soaked dal in 3 to 4 changes of water until the washing water is relatively clear. Drain in a strainer. Place the dal and ⅔ cup of the water into a blender. Grind to a fine paste. In a large bowl, add the cream of rice and remaining ⅓ cup water. Mix well. Add the dal paste to the cream of rice. Add the salt and stir thoroughly

Cover and keep in a warm place for 20 to 24 hours. The dough will ferment and almost double in size. (I usually ferment it overnight and steam it the next night for dinner.) Stir the fermented mixture very gently to mix the top and bottom, using a folding motion.

Brush or spray idli containers (see Note, below) with oil. Fill the idli containers to the top line of the indentation, about ¼ cup each, or pour the batter into 2 oiled 6- to 8-inch round or square cake pans. Bring ½ to 1 cup water to a boil in a pan that holds the idli container or cake pans. Once water is boiling, add the filled idli containers or cake pans with tongs and cover with a lid. Reduce the heat and steam for 10 minutes. Remove the idli containers and cool slightly. Using a butter knife, remove the idlies and place in a container lined with a towel. Wrap with the towel to keep them warm. If using the cake pans, cut the idlies into 24 equal pieces.

Idli containers are round pans with indentations similar to an egg poacher; they can be stacked so you can steam several idlies at a time.

CHICKEN-RICE CASSEROLE
Murgh Biriyani

This is a very popular dish made on special occasions. Here is a much lower-fat version of the biriyani. Serve with salad and Cilanto Chutney (page 209) for a great meal.

1 ½ cups basmati rice

1 pound boneless, skinless, chicken

2 tablespoons vegetable oil

½ teaspoon cumin seeds

4 cardamom pods

8 black peppercorns

4 whole cloves

1-inch stick cinnamon

2 bay leaves

1 medium onion, finely sliced

2 garlic cloves, crushed

1 teaspoon chopped fresh ginger

¼ teaspoon turmeric

1 cup plain nonfat yogurt

2 teaspoons salt

3 ½ cups water

Clean the rice, removing any unhulled rice or other extraneous material. Wash in 2 to 3 changes of water until the washing water is relatively clear. Soak in cold water for ½ hour or longer. (Soaking helps make the rice grains longer. If you don't have time, this soaking can be eliminated.) Drain the rice in a strainer.

Cut the chicken into bite-size pieces.

Heat the oil in a heavy skillet over medium-high heat. Add the cumin seeds, cardamom pods, black peppercorns, cloves, cinnamon stick and bay leaves.

Fry until the cumin seeds are golden brown, a few seconds. Add the onion, garlic and ginger. Fry until the onion is soft and transparent.

Add the chicken pieces and fry 3 to 4 minutes, until the chicken turns white and firm, stirring frequently. Add the turmeric and stir to mix.

Beat the yogurt with a fork. Add to the chicken gradually, 1 to 2 tablespoons at a time, stirring constantly. Cook over high heat until most of the liquid is evaporated and the yogurt masala clings to the chicken. Add the salt and water. Bring to a boil, cover with a lid and reduce the heat; simmer for 5 to 7 minutes.

Add the rice, bring to a boil, reduce the heat and cover with a lid. Simmer until the water is absorbed and rice is done, 15 to 17 minutes. Let stand, covered, until ready to serve.

MAKES 12
(½-CUP) SERVINGS

PER SERVING

Calories 106

Carbohydrate 20 g

Fat 1 g

Saturated fat 0 g

Dietary fiber 1.2 g

Protein 4 g

Cholesterol 0 mg

Sodium 269 mg

EXCHANGES

1 starch

1 lean meat

RICE AND BEAN PORRIDGE
Kheechri

Kheechri is a light meal often served like a porridge. Moong dal is considered to be the easiest pulse to digest. It tastes great served with pickles, roasted Papad (page 61) and plain yogurt. This kheechri is best when slightly overcooked. You can still see the rice and dal grain but it should be well blended and have a porridge-like consistency.

1 cup long-grain rice

¾ cup split moong (page 106)

2 teaspoons ghee

Pinch of asafetida

½ teaspoon cumin seeds

½ teaspoon turmeric

1 ½ teaspoons salt

5 cups water

Clean the rice and moong dal of any extraneous material. Combine them and wash in 2 to 3 changes of water, until the washing water is relatively clear. Drain in a strainer and set aside.

Heat the ghee in heavy skillet over medium-high heat. Add the asafetida and cumin seeds and cook until the cumin seeds are golden brown, a few seconds. Add the rice mixture, turmeric, salt and water. Bring to a boil. Reduce the heat and cover with a lid, leaving it ajar to avoid boiling over. Simmer for 30 to 35 minutes, stirring occasionally. Serve hot.

DALS

Dal is technically a dried, dehusked, split bean. But the word *dal* in India is used loosely for all pulses (legumes). The pulses are used in all their different forms. They are used as a whole bean, split with husk, split without husk and polished (commonly known as washed) or ground into flour. Most of the *dals* are available in stores that carry Indian groceries. Local supermarkets also have some *dals* but usually only the whole variety, for example, chickpeas, brown lentils and kidney beans.

Dals are used extensively in the Indian diet. For vegetarians, *dals* provide the essential protein. For centuries, Indians have combined *dal* and rice or bread for the main course. *Dal* is often the main dish, so to speak. A vegetarian meal is often planned around what goes best with the particular *dal*, similar to a nonvegetarian meal being planned around what goes best with a particular meat. *Dals* are very versatile. Most have a mild but distinct taste and texture. The variety of dishes made with *dals* in India is unlimited and includes main courses, snacks and desserts.

COMMON *DALS* USED IN INDIA

Chana dal (*Bengal gram*): This is the split, polished variety of the bengal *gram* bean. This looks like yellow split peas but it is smaller and sweeter in flavor. It is used in many recipes other than just as a soup or *dal*. For example, it is used as a seasoning in many south Indian dishes and adds a nutlike flavor. It is also ground to make a flour known as *besan*. The whole bean (*kala chana*) looks similar to a chickpea but is smaller, has a black husk and has a different taste.

Chickpeas (garbanzo beans, kabuli chana): I prefer to use the dried chickpeas. I will sometimes use the canned chickpeas for convenience.

Chickpea flour: See *besan* (page 35).

Kidney beans (rajmah): I usually use the dried red kidney beans. On occasion I will substitute canned ones for convenience.

Black-eyed peas (lobhia): These are also known as cowpeas. Use the dried black-eyed peas for better flavor or canned ones for convenience.

Lentils (masoor dal): Lentils are used whole or split and polished. The whole *masoor* (*sabut masoor*) is sold as lentils in the United States. The polished, split variety (*dhuli masoor*) is salmon colored and may be sold as split lentils.

Moong dal (green gram): *Moong dal* is sold whole, split with the skin or dehusked and polished. Each type of *moong dal* has a distinct taste, so use the one the recipe calls for.

Toor dal (pigeon peas or arhar dal): *Toor dal* is sold split and polished only. It comes from a red *gram* whole bean, but the whole variety is rarely used. *Toor dal* is sold as regular or oily. I prefer the regular type but you can wash the oily one in hot water to remove the oil.

Urad dal (black gram): This *dal* is sold whole, split with the skin or split and polished. Each type has a distinct use in a recipe, so notice which one the recipe calls for.

COOKING DALS

Cooking *dals* takes time, especially whole *dals*. Most Indians use pressure cookers for cooking *dals*, because they save significant amounts of cooking time. I have included the amount of time needed to cook *dals* using the pressure cooker. If you have never used a pressure cooker, see "Using the Pressure Cooker" (page 30).

Soaking also cuts down on cooking time, but *dals* can be cooked without soaking. Soaking especially helps with whole beans like kidney beans or chickpeas (garbanzo beans). The split and dehusked varieties take the least amount of time to cook.

EATING BEANS

In the United States, people often associate beans with bloating and stomach discomfort. This discourages them from using beans in their diet. In India beans have been a staple for centuries. The use of spices and seasonings reduces the discomfort associated with beans and *dals* by aiding the digestive process. Asafetida, turmeric, ginger, onions and garlic all improve the digestibility of beans.

If you are not used to eating beans, start with a small serving and increase it gradually as you build tolerance.

Exchanges are calculated based on the carbohydrate and protein content. The calories may be less than the computed exchanges because beans are high in protein and carbohydrates.

BLACK-EYED PEAS
Sukha Lobhia

MAKES 4
(½-CUP) SERVINGS

PER SERVING

Calories 88

Carbohydrate 13 g

Fat 1.5 g

Saturated fat 0 g

Dietary fiber 5 g

Protein 6 g

Cholesterol 0 mg

Sodium 270 mg

EXCHANGES

1 starch

1 lean meat

Lobhia, or black-eyed peas, are cooked in variety of ways. My quick version uses canned peas, but dried black-eyed peas can be used, soaked and cooked until tender. This dish is great as a snack or a side dish.

1 (16-ounce) can black-eyed peas

1 teaspoon vegetable oil

Pinch of asafetida

¼ teaspoon cumin seeds

¼ teaspoon turmeric

¼ teaspoon cayenne pepper (optional)

1 teaspoon coriander powder

½ teaspoon salt

½ cup water

¼ teaspoon Garam Masala (page 48) or purchased

1 teaspoon fresh lemon juice

In a strainer, drain and rinse the black-eyed peas. Set aside.

In a heavy nonstick skillet, heat the oil over medium heat. Add the asafetida and cumin seeds. Cook until the cumin seeds are golden brown, a few seconds. Add the black-eyed peas and stir. Add the turmeric, cayenne pepper (if using), coriander powder, salt and water. Stir to mix.

Bring to a boil. Cover with a lid and reduce the heat. Simmer until most of the water is absorbed, 10 to 12 minutes.

Add the garam masala and lemon juice and stir to combine. Transfer to a serving platter.

PIGEON PEAS
Toor Dal

PER SERVING
Calories 90
Carbohydrate 15 g
Fat 1 g
Saturated fat 0 g
Dietary fiber 3 g
Protein 5 g
Cholesterol 0 mg
Sodium 271 mg

EXCHANGES
1 starch
½ lean meat

Toor dal is the most versatile dal. This plain version is nice because it is easy and can be served with any spicy vegetable. Its mild flavor combines well with other side dishes without clashing.

1 cup toor dal

4 cups water

1 teaspoon salt

¼ teaspoon turmeric

1 teaspoon vegetable oil

Pinch of asafetida

¼ teaspoon cumin seeds

1 teaspoon coriander powder

1 tablespoon chopped cilantro (optional)

Clean the toor dal of any extraneous materials. Wash the dal in 2 to 3 changes of water.

In a heavy skillet, add the toor dal, water, salt and turmeric. Bring to a boil over medium-high heat. Reduce the heat, cover with a lid and simmer until tender and soupy, 30 to 40 minutes. (The dal and water should not separate.)

To cook in a pressure cooker, put the cleaned dal, 3 cups of water, salt and turmeric in the pressure cooker. Seal and put the weight in place. Cook on medium-high heat until pressure develops, reduce the heat and cook under pressure for 5 minutes. Cool the cooker to remove the pressure. Open the lid carefully. Return to the heat and simmer until the dal is of desired consistency as stated above.

To prepare the chounk (seasoning): In a small frying pan, heat the oil to near the smoking point. Add the asafetida and cumin seeds and cook until the cumin seeds are golden brown, a few seconds. Remove from the heat and add the coriander powder. Immediately add to the dal and stir.

Transfer to a serving platter, garnish with the cilantro, if desired. Serve hot. Dal thickens as it cools.

SPROUTED MOONG

MAKES 6
(½-CUP) SERVINGS

PER SERVING
Calories 122
Carbohydrate 20 g
Fat 1 g
Saturated fat 0 g
Protein 8 g
Dietary fiber 2.7 g
Cholesterol 0 mg
Sodium 272 mg

EXCHANGES
1 starch
1 lean meat

This is very popular way to prepare moong, or moth dal as it is called in my husband's home (Rajasthan). You need to plan ahead as it takes two to three days to soak and sprout the dal. I have at times sprouted enough for two to three meals and frozen the sprouted dal. Once sprouted it cooks very quickly. My children love this served over rice with a little ghee and sugar sprinkled on top (of course, that is how my husband eats it too).

1 cup whole moong dal

1 teaspoon vegetable oil

Pinch of asafetida

½ teaspoon cumin seeds

¼ teaspoon turmeric

1 teaspoon coriander powder

¼ teaspoon cayenne pepper (optional)

¾ teaspoon salt

¾ cup water

Clean the moong dal of any extraneous materials. Wash in 2 to 3 changes of water. Cover with water and soak overnight.

Drain the moong. Wrap drained moong in a cloth (an old kitchen towel or a strainer works well) and place in a bowl. Pour ½ cup water over the cloth to keep the moong and cloth moist and cover with a lid. Keep in a warm place like the oven for 24 to 36 hours or until about ¼-inch sprouts form. (To speed the process I sometimes turn on the oven light.)

Place the sprouted moong in a strainer and rinse with fresh water. Heat the oil in a heavy pan over medium-high heat. Add the asafetida and the cumin seeds. Fry until golden brown, a few seconds.

Add the sprouted moong, turmeric, coriander powder, cayenne pepper, (if using), salt and water and stir. Bring to a boil. Cover, reduce the heat and simmer until soft to the touch but still firm, 20 to 30 minutes.

Remove the lid, increase the heat and evaporate any excess water accumulated at the bottom. Transfer to a serving bowl.

LENTIL SOUP

Masoor Dal

MAKES 8
(½-CUP) SERVINGS

PER SERVING

Calories 90

Carbohydrate 14 g

Fat 0.8 g

Saturated fat 0 g

Dietary fiber 4.5 g

Protein 7 g

Cholesterol 0 mg

Sodium 269 mg

EXCHANGES

1 starch

1 lean meat

To get the best flavor of this dal, cook until the water and dal do not separate. Serve it over rice or with any good bread.

> 1 cup lentils (whole masoor)
>
> 6 cups water
>
> 1 teaspoon salt
>
> ½ teaspoon turmeric
>
> 1 teaspoon vegetable oil
>
> Pinch of asafetida
>
> ½ teaspoon cumin seeds
>
> 1 teaspoon fresh lemon juice

Clean the lentils of any extraneous material. Wash in 2 to 3 changes of water.

In a medium saucepan, combine the lentils, water, salt and turmeric. Bring to a boil over high heat. Reduce the heat, cover tightly with a lid and simmer until the lentils are very soft, about 1½ hours.

To cook in a pressure cooker put the lentils, 4 cups of water, salt and turmeric in a pressure cooker. Cover with a lid and put the pressure weight in place. Cook over medium heat until pressure develops, reduce the heat and cook under pressure for 20 minutes. Cool completely before opening the pressure cooker. Return to the heat and continue to simmer until desired consistency. For best results cook the lentils until the beans and water do not separate.

To prepare chounk (seasoning): In a small frying pan, heat the oil to near the smoking point. Add the asafetida and cumin seeds. Fry until the cumin seeds are golden brown, for a few seconds. Add to the dal.

Add the lemon juice and stir to combine. Transfer to a serving bowl.

WHOLE URAD DAL
Dal Makhani

This is the dal most commonly served in restaurants in the United States. In restaurants, the chefs cook it with cream to give it a very smooth, rich taste. I use milk and find that the longer you cook it, the creamier and mellower the taste becomes. Serve with rice or any roti or bread of your choice.

¾ cup whole urad dal

2 tablespoons dried black-eyed peas

9 cups water

1 teaspoon salt

½ teaspoon turmeric

1 tablespoon chopped fresh ginger

4 teaspoons vegetable oil

Pinch of asafetida

½ teaspoon cumin seeds

1 cup thinly sliced onion

2 teaspoons coriander powder

½ teaspoon cayenne pepper (optional)

1 cup skim milk

Clean the urad dal and black-eyed peas of any extraneous materials. Wash in 2 to 3 changes of water.

Add the dal and peas to the water, salt, turmeric and ginger in a heavy 4-quart saucepan and bring to a boil over high heat. Reduce the heat and simmer until the dal is done and the water and beans do not separate, 3 to 3½ hours. The long cooking time gives it a reddish brown color and a creamy taste. Add more water if it becomes too thick.

To cook in a pressure cooker, add the dal, 6 cups water, salt, turmeric and ginger. Seal and put the pressure weight in place. Cook over medium-high heat until the pressure develops. Reduce the heat and cook under pressure for 45 minutes. Cool the cooker until the pressure is removed. Open the lid carefully. Stir, checking for consistency as above. If the dal is not well blended, return to the heat and cook under pressure again for 10 to 15 minutes.

To prepare onion masala, heat the oil in a nonstick frying pan on medium-high heat. Add the asafetida and cumin seeds and cook until the cumin seeds are golden brown, a few seconds. Add the onion. Stir constantly, frying until it is golden brown. Remove from the heat. Add the coriander and cayenne pepper (if using). Add the onion masala and milk to the boiled beans. Bring to boil, reduce the heat and cook for 10 to 15 minutes to desired consistency.

Transfer to a serving platter and serve hot.

KIDNEY BEANS
Rajmah

PER SERVING

Calories 125

Carbohydrate 17 g

Fat 3.5 g

Saturated fat 0 g

Dietary fiber 7.4 g

Protein 6 g

Cholesterol 0 mg

Sodium 278 mg

EXCHANGES

1 starch

1 lean meat

Rajmah is a specialty of the state of Punjab. Kidney beans take a long time to cook, but with a pressure cooker the time is reduced drastically. When in a hurry, use drained and rinsed canned kidney beans; substitute two cans for one cup of dry beans. Serve with rice or roti (page 78).

1 cup dried kidney beans

6 cups water

1 teaspoon salt

¼ teaspoon turmeric

1 medium tomato

1 medium onion

1 tablespoon chopped fresh ginger

½ teaspoon cumin seeds

2 tablespoons vegetable oil

⅓ cup plain nonfat yogurt

2 teaspoons coriander powder

½ teaspoon cayenne pepper (optional)

½ teaspoon Garam Masala (page 48) or purchased

2 tablespoons chopped cilantro

Clean the kidney beans and remove any extraneous materials. Wash in 2 to 3 changes of water. Soak overnight in 4 cups of the water.

In a heavy saucepan, add the kidney beans and the soaking water plus the remaining 2 cups of water and the salt. Bring to a boil over high heat. Reduce the heat, cover with a lid and simmer until the beans are very tender, about 2 hours. The kidney beans should be slightly split and should mash easily with a spoon against the side of the pan.

To cook in a pressure cooker, add the kidney beans with the soaking water and salt. Do not add the additional 2 cups of water. Seal and put the pressure weight in place. Cook over medium heat until the pressure develops.

Reduce the heat and cook under pressure for 20 minutes. Cool the cooker until the pressure is removed. Open the lid carefully. Check the beans for tenderness as described above.

In the meantime, grind the tomato, onion, ginger and cumin seeds in a blender to a smooth paste. Set aside.

In a nonstick frying pan, add the onion paste. Cook over medium-high heat, stirring occasionally, until all the water evaporates. Add the oil and continue to fry until the onion masala is light brown.

Lightly beat the yogurt and add it, 1 tablespoon at a time, to the onion masala as it cooks. Add the coriander powder and cayenne pepper (if using). Fry the mixture, stirring constantly, until most of the liquid in the pan evaporates and the mixture is thick enough to draw away from the sides and bottom of the pan in a dense mass.

Add the onion mixture to the boiled beans and stir thoroughly. Bring to a boil. Reduce the heat and simmer for 10 minutes. Stir in the garam masala and 1 tablespoon of the cilantro. Remove from the heat.

Transfer to a serving dish and garnish with the remaining cilantro.

CHANA DAL WITH BOTTLE GOURD

Chana Dal aur Lauki

MAKES 8
(½-CUP) SERVINGS

PER SERVING

Calories 100

Carbohydrate 15 g

Fat 2 g

Saturated fat 0 g

Dietary fiber 7 g

Protein 5 g

Cholesterol 0 mg

Sodium 298 mg

EXCHANGES

1 starch

½ lean meat

Traditionally, this dal is cooked with lauki (bottle gourd). In the summer I do use lauki, often available in specialty stores. Celery, however, makes a nice substitute and is available all year.

1 cup chana dal

6 cups water

1 teaspoon salt

½ teaspoon turmeric

1 cup peeled and diced bottle gourd or celery (½-inch pieces)

1 teaspoon vegetable oil

Pinch of asafetida

¼ teaspoon cumin seeds

2 teaspoons fresh lemon juice, or to taste

Clean the chana dal of any extraneous materials. Wash chana dal in 3 to 4 changes of water. Set aside.

To a medium saucepan, add the chana dal, water, salt and turmeric. Bring to a boil over medium-high heat. Reduce the heat, cover with a lid, leaving it ajar, and simmer for 1 to 1½ hours until the dal is very soft and turning soupy. Beat with an egg beater or a wire whisk 2 to 3 times to blend the dal into the water. The dal and water should not separate.

To cook in a pressure cooker, put the chana dal, 4 cups of water, the salt and turmeric in a pressure cooker. Seal and put the pressure weight in place. Cook over medium-high heat until the pressure develops. Reduce the heat and cook under pressure for 15 minutes. Cool until the pressure is removed. Open the lid carefully. Check for desired consistency and beat as mentioned above. Return to the heat.

Add the bottle gourd or celery and simmer until the vegetable is tender, 10 to 12 minutes.

To prepare the chounk (seasoning): In a small frying pan, heat the oil to near the smoking point. Add the asafetida and cumin seeds and cook until the cumin seeds are golden brown, a few seconds. Add the chounk to the dal.

Remove from the heat, add the lemon juice and stir. Transfer to a serving dish.

SWEET AND SOUR DAL

Gujrati Dal

MAKES 8
(½-CUP) SERVINGS

PER SERVING

Calories 80

Carbohydrate 14 g

Fat 1 g

Saturated fat 0 g

Dietary fiber 2.5 g

Protein 4 g

Cholesterol 0 mg

Sodium 271 mg

EXCHANGE

1 starch

½ lean meat

This is a sweet and sour toor dal, a specialty of the state of Gujarat. It tastes great with rice or as a soup.

¾ cup toor dal

4 cups water

1 teaspoon salt

¼ teaspoon turmeric

1 large tomato

4 teaspoons sugar

1 tablespoon fresh lemon juice

1 teaspoon vegetable oil

Pinch of asafetida

¼ teaspoon brown mustard seeds

4 to 6 curry leaves

1 tablespoon chopped cilantro (optional)

Clean the toor dal of any extraneous materials. Wash in 3 to 4 changes of water.

To a saucepan, add the toor dal, water, salt, turmeric and the whole tomato. Bring to a boil over high heat. Reduce the heat, cover with a lid and simmer until the dal is tender and soupy, 45 to 60 minutes. (The dal and water should not separate.)

To cook in a pressure cooker, put the dal, 3 cups of water, salt, turmeric and the whole tomato in a pressure cooker. Seal and put the pressure weight in place. Cook over medium heat until the pressure develops. Reduce the heat and cook under pressure for 5 minutes. Cool until the pressure is removed. Open the lid carefully. Return to the heat and continue to simmer until it reaches the right consistency, as described above.

Take out the tomato and pass it through a sieve, saving the juice. Add the tomato juice to the dal and stir; discard the seeds and skin. Lightly beat the dal with a wire whisk or egg beater, 2 to 3 times only, to blend the dal.

Add the sugar and lemon juice; stir gently to combine.

To prepare the chounk (seasoning): Heat the oil in a small frying pan over medium-high heat. Add the asafetida and mustard seeds, cover with a lid to avoid splattering and fry until the mustard seeds stop popping, a few seconds. Remove from the heat, add the curry leaves and fry for a few seconds. Add the chounk to the dal; stir to combine.

Transfer to a serving platter, garnish with the cilantro, if desired, and serve hot.

CHICKPEA SOUP
Kaddi

MAKES 9
(¾-CUP) SERVINGS

PER SERVING
Calories 117
Carbohydrate 13 g
Fat 5 g
Saturated fat 0.5 g
Dietary fiber 4.3 g
Protein 5.6 g
Cholesterol 0 mg
Sodium 397 mg

EXCHANGES
1 milk
1 fat

Kaddi is a very popular dish throughout northern India. It is prepared in various ways, but this is the most common version in my home. It is often made with sour yogurt. It can be prepared with fresh yogurt, using lemon juice to add the sour taste. Serve it with rice.

1 ½ cups plain nonfat yogurt (see Note, below)

1 ½ cups besan (chickpea flour), sifted

5 ⅓ cups water

½ teaspoon turmeric

½ teaspoon cayenne pepper (optional)

1 ½ teaspoons salt

2 teaspoons vegetable oil

Pinch of asafetida

¼ teaspoon fenugreek seeds

¼ teaspoon cumin seeds

2 dried whole red chiles

Vegetable oil, for frying

2 teaspoons fresh lemon juice, plus extra for serving

Mix the yogurt, ¾ cup of the besan, 5 cups of the water, the turmeric, cayenne pepper (if using) and 1 teaspoon of the salt. Set aside.

In a large heavy saucepan, heat the oil to near the smoking point; add the asafetida, fenugreek seeds, cumin seeds and red chiles. Cook until the cumin seeds are golden brown, a few seconds. Add the yogurt mixture and stir to combine. Bring to a boil over medium-high heat, stirring frequently. The mixture may boil over, so watch carefully and stir as needed. Reduce the heat, partially cover with a lid and simmer for 30 minutes, stirring occasionally.

In the meantime, mix the remaining ¾ cup besan and the remaining ⅓ cup water. Beat with a hand or electric mixer until light and fluffy. To test the mixture, drop a small amount of blended besan paste into a cup of cold water. The paste should float to the top. If it does not, continue to beat with mixer and repeat the test. When the paste floats to the top, beat in the remaining ½ teaspoon salt. Set aside.

In a medium frying pan or wok, heat 1 inch of oil over high heat until very hot. Make pakories (besan balls), using a teaspoon or your fingertips, add about 1 teaspoon of besan paste at a time to the hot oil. Add as many balls as the frying pan will hold in a single layer. Fry on one side until light brown, turn over and fry the other side. Drain on paper towels. Repeat process until all the besan paste is used.

To a medium bowl, add about 2 cups very hot water. Add the pakories and soak for 10 to 20 minutes.

Drain the pakories and add them to the soup. Simmer for 5 minutes. Stir in lemon juice.

Transfer to a serving bowl. Serve with additional lemon juice to accommodate individual tastes.

NOTE

For the best results, use sour yogurt left at room temperature overnight.

TOOR DAL WITH VEGETABLES
Sambhar

MAKES 10
(½-CUP) SERVINGS

PER SERVING

Calories 86

Carbohydrate 15 g

Fat 1 g

Saturated fat 0 g

Dietary fiber 3.2 g

Protein 5 g

EXCHANGES

1 starch

½ lean meat

There are as many ways to cook this as there are cooks. This is a very popular way to cook dal throughout southern India. Serve with Steamed Rice Dumplings (Idli, page 100) or rice.

1 cup toor dal

6 cups water

1½ teaspoons salt

½ teaspoon turmeric

1 medium onion, chopped into ½-inch pieces

1 medium tomato, chopped into 1-inch cubes

½ cup sliced carrot

½ cup chopped green beans

3 tablespoons Sambhar Powder (page 50)

1 teaspoon tamarind concentrate

2 teaspoons vegetable oil

Pinch of asafetida

½ teaspoon brown mustard seeds

6 to 8 curry leaves

Clean the toor dal of any extraneous materials. Wash in 2 to 3 changes of water.

To a heavy saucepan, add the toor dal, water, salt and turmeric. Bring to a boil over high heat. Reduce the heat; cover with a lid and simmer until the dal is tender and soupy, 45 to 50 minutes. (The dal and water should not separate.)

To cook in a pressure cooker, put the dal, 4 cups of water, salt and turmeric in the cooker. Seal and put the pressure weight in place. Cook over medium heat until pressure develops. Reduce the heat and cook under pressure for 5 minutes. Cool until the pressure is removed. Open the lid carefully. Return to the heat and simmer until it reaches the consistency described above.

In the meantime, chop the vegetables. When the dal is well done, add the onion, tomato, carrot, green beans and sambhar powder. Bring to a boil, reduce the heat and simmer until the vegetables are tender, about 10 minutes.

Add the tamarind concentrate and continue to simmer while preparing the seasoning.

To prepare the chounk (seasoning): Heat the oil in a small frying pan over medium heat. Add the asafetida and mustard seeds, cover with a lid to avoid splattering and cook until the mustard seeds stop popping, a few seconds. Remove from the heat, add the curry leaves and return to the heat for a few seconds. Add the chounk to the dal mixture and stir to combine.

Transfer to a serving bowl and serve hot.

SPICY CHICKPEAS
Chole

MAKES 8
(½-CUP) SERVINGS

PER SERVING
Calories 161
Carbohydrate 24 g
Fat 4 g
Saturated fat 0 g
Dietary fiber 11.6 g
Protein 7 g
Cholesterol 0 mg
Sodium 415 mg

EXCHANGES
1 starch
1 medium-fat meat

Chole is becoming a very popular dish all over India. It originates from the state of Punjab, and in north India it is available at most restaurants. Many street vendors sell chole with puri or bhatura (fried breads). People eat them as a meal or a snack. It is usually served hot but is also great cold for picnics. The most popular version is made in a tamarind sauce and is fairly spicy (not necessarily chile hot). For best results, use dry chickpeas and cook them until they are very soft. The flavor of the dish improves as the spices blend with the chickpeas. I usually cook this three to four hours before I want to serve it.

1½ cups dried chickpeas (garbanzo beans)

6 cups water

1½ teaspoons salt

2 × 1-inch piece dry tamarind or 1 teaspoon tamarind concentrate

½ cup boiling water

4 teaspoons vegetable oil

½ teaspoon cumin seeds

2 whole cloves

2 bay leaves

1-inch cinnamon stick

1 cup thinly sliced onion

2 garlic cloves (optional)

1 teaspoon chopped fresh ginger

½ cup chopped tomato

1 tablespoon coriander powder

1½ teaspoons Garam Masala (page 48) or purchased

½ teaspoon cayenne pepper (optional)

1 small hot green chile, chopped (optional)

2 tablespoons chopped cilantro

Clean the chickpeas and remove any extraneous materials. Wash chickpeas in 2 to 3 changes of water. Soak overnight in 4 cups of the water.

In a heavy saucepan, add the chickpeas and the soaking water plus the remaining 2 cups of water and the salt. Bring to a boil over high heat. As white froth develops, skim with a large slotted spoon and discard. Reduce the heat; cover with a lid and simmer until the beans are very tender, about 2 hours. The chickpeas should be slightly split and should mash easily with a spoon against the side of the pan. As you stir, the chickpeas should be soft enough to fall apart.

To cook in a pressure cooker, pour in the chickpeas and the soaking water and the salt. (Do not add the additional 2 cups of water.) Bring to a boil over high heat. Skim the white froth and discard. Seal and put the pressure weight in place. Once the pressure develops, reduce the heat and cook under pressure for 30 minutes. Cool the cooker until all the pressure is removed. Open the lid carefully. Check the beans for tenderness, as indicated above.

In the meantime, soak the dry tamarind in the boiling water. Let stand for 20 minutes or longer. Squeeze the tamarind with your fingers and thumb to remove the juice. Strain the juice and discard the pulp, as you will only use the tamarind juice. Set aside. If you are using the tamarind concentrate, mix with boiling water and set aside.

Heat the oil in a nonstick frying pan over medium-high heat. Add the cumin seeds, cloves, bay leaves and cinnamon stick. Fry until the cumin seeds are golden brown, a few seconds. Add the onion, garlic (if using) and ginger and cook until the onion is golden brown, stirring frequently. Reduce the heat; add the tomato and cook until it is tender, 2 to 5 minutes, stirring frequently.

Add the onion-spice mixture, coriander powder, garam masala, cayenne pepper (if using) and chile (if using) to the boiled chickpeas. Add the tamarind and stir thoroughly. Bring to a boil. Reduce the heat, cover and simmer for 30 minutes, stirring occasionally.

Transfer to a serving platter. Garnish with the cilantro.

MAKES 6
(½-CUP) SERVINGS

PER SERVING

Calories 123

Carbohydrate 20 g

Fat 1 g

Saturated fat 0 g

Dietary fiber 1.7 g

Protein 8 g

Cholesterol 0 mg

Sodium 364 mg

EXCHANGES

1 starch

1 lean meat

DRY MOONG DAL

Sukhi Moong Dal

This dal is cooked until just tender and served dry instead of soupy like most dals. It goes great with roti (page 78) or rice. Sometimes my mother would serve it with milk as an after-school snack.

1 cup dehusked moong dal (yellow)

1 ½ cups water

¼ teaspoon turmeric

1 teaspoon salt

2 teaspoons vegetable oil

Pinch of asafetida

¼ teaspoon cumin seeds

½ teaspoon cayenne pepper (optional)

2 teaspoons coriander powder

½ teaspoon Garam Masala (page 48) or purchased

2 teaspoons fresh lemon juice

Clean the moong dal of any extraneous materials. Wash in 3 to 4 changes of water.

To a medium saucepan, add the moong dal, water, turmeric and salt. Bring to a boil. Reduce the heat, cover with a lid and simmer for 12 to 15 minutes. Do not overcook the dal. (The dal should be tender to touch but intact.) Remove from the heat and set aside.

To prepare the chounk (seasoning): Heat the oil in a large nonstick frying pan over medium heat. Add the asafetida and cumin seeds and cook until the cumin seeds are golden brown, a few seconds. Add the cooked dal to the chounk. Add the cayenne pepper (if using), coriander powder, garam masala and lemon juice. Stir carefully with a spatula to avoid mashing or breaking the dal. Cook for 5 to 7 minutes, stirring occasionally, allowing any liquid that has accumulated to evaporate. Transfer to a serving platter.

VEGETABLES

Indians generally love vegetables. Because of the tropical climate, the variety of vegetables available in India is much more extensive than in the colder climates of the Western world. Large numbers of Indians are vegetarians so they have created limitless ways of preparing vegetables. Vegetables are never just boiled; spices are used to add flavor and variety.

The vegetables are either cooked dry (*sukhi subji*) or in a sauce (*tari subji*). The preparation of vegetables varies from state to state and from household to household. Some recipes may call for cooking the vegetables just enough to make them tender, whereas others may require them to be simmered until the vegetables are soft and well blended with the spices.

When in a hurry, I often use frozen vegetables. I also use my food processor to grate or chop vegetables if possible. I rarely use canned vegetables except tomato sauce, chopped tomatoes and sometimes dried beans or new potatoes. Even in a hurry I use all the spices the dish calls for. Whether you use one spice or six it takes the same amount of time. The spices add flavor, variety and taste.

Vegetables are usually cooked in a fair amount of oil, either fried or roasted with spices. I have found the amount of oil needed to bring out the flavor and taste can be drastically reduced. Over the years I have successfully reduced the amount of oil used in dishes without compromising the taste. A minimum amount of oil is used to roast or fry the spices. Use a nonstick pan for the dry vegetables (*sukhi subji*). Although the prepared vegetables are not fat free, the amount of fat is very low.

If you thought vegetables were boring, hold on and give your palate a real treat!

CAULIFLOWER MIXED VEGETABLES

Gobhi Gajar Ki Subji

This is one of my family's favorite vegetable dishes. It is colorful and has a nice blend of flavors. Cauliflower is typically fried or cooked in a fair amount of oil, but I add the oil at the end, to bring a similar flavor with a fraction of the fat.

1 small cauliflower, divided into 1-inch florets (3 cups)

1½ cups carrot slices (¼ inch)

1½ cups zucchini slices (¼ inch)

4 teaspoons vegetable oil

Pinch of asafetida (optional)

½ teaspoon cumin seeds

1 teaspoon chopped fresh ginger

¼ teaspoon turmeric

1½ teaspoons salt

½ teaspoon cayenne pepper (optional)

1 tablespoon coriander powder

½ teaspoon mango powder

¾ teaspoon Garam Masala (page 48) or purchased

1 tablespoon chopped cilantro

Wash and drain the cauliflower, carrots and zucchini. Set aside.

Heat 1 teaspoon of the oil in a heavy, nonstick skillet over medium-high heat. Add the asafetida (if using) and cumin seeds and cook until the seeds are golden brown, a few seconds.

Add the vegetables and stir. Add the ginger, turmeric, salt and cayenne pepper (if using) and stir to coat the vegetables. Cook until hot. Cover with a lid and reduce the heat. Simmer until the vegetables are tender but firm, 8 to 10 minutes, stirring once or twice.

Sprinkle with the coriander powder, mango powder and garam masala. Stir carefully in a lifting and turning fashion so you do not mash the vegetables.

Add the remaining 3 teaspoons of oil around the sides of the pan, allowing the oil to flow to the bottom of the pan. All the liquid from the vegetables should be evaporated; if not, increase the heat and cook to evaporate it. Fry for 3 to 5 minutes, stirring once or twice in the same lifting and turning fashion. This final roasting or frying in the oil brings out the true flavor of this dish.

Transfer to a serving platter. Garnish with the cilantro.

SPICY NEW POTATOES

Jeera Alu

MAKES 6
(½-CUP) SERVINGS

PER SERVING

Calories 95

Carbohydrate 13 g

Fat 5 g

Saturated fat 0.5 g

Dietary fiber 2.3 g

Protein 1 g

Cholesterol 0 mg

Sodium 35 mg

EXCHANGES

1 starch

1 fat

My mother made these with small new potatoes fresh out of the garden. I use the canned potatoes because they are convenient and always available. If you choose to use fresh new potatoes, steam them first and follow the directions.

2 (16-ounce) cans whole new potatoes

2 tablespoons vegetable oil

½ teaspoon cumin seeds

¼ teaspoon turmeric

1 teaspoon salt

1 tablespoon coriander powder

¼ teaspoon cayenne pepper (optional)

½ teaspoon mango powder

1 teaspoon Garam Masala (page 48) or purchased

Drain and rinse the potatoes. Cut any potatoes larger than 1 inch into half.

Heat the oil in a heavy frying pan or a wok over medium heat. Add the cumin seeds and cook until the seeds turn golden brown, a few seconds. Add the potatoes and stir to coat.

Add the remaining spices and stir to combine. Reduce the heat and fry for 15 to 20 minutes, stirring occasionally. Transfer to a serving platter.

MAKES 6
(½-CUP) SERVINGS

PER SERVING
Calories 90
Carbohydrate 19 g
Fat 1 g
Saturated fat 0 g
Dietary fiber 2 g
Protein 2 g
Cholesterol 0 g
Sodium 410 mg

EXCHANGE
1 starch

POTATO AND PEA CURRY
Alu Matar

A favorite of children and adults alike, this vegetable dish goes with everything. The curry sauce can be thin or fairly thick, depending on what you are in the mood for or what else is being served. I use tomato sauce for convenience. Substitute a large tomato, if desired.

3 medium potatoes

1 teaspoon vegetable oil

¼ teaspoon cumin seeds

¾ cup frozen or fresh green peas

½ cup tomato sauce or 1 large tomato, ground

½ teaspoon turmeric

2 teaspoons coriander powder

¼ teaspoon cayenne pepper (optional)

¾ teaspoon salt

2½ cups water

½ teaspoon Garam Masala (page 48) or purchased

1 tablespoon chopped cilantro

Peel and wash the potatoes. Cut into 1½-inch pieces. Set aside.

Heat the oil in a heavy saucepan over medium heat. Add cumin seeds and cook until the seeds are golden brown, a few seconds.

Add the potatoes, peas and tomato sauce; stir to combine. Add the turmeric, coriander powder and cayenne pepper (if using). Stirring constantly, cook until the tomato sauce is dry and coats the potatoes.

Add the salt and water. Bring to a boil. Reduce the heat, cover with a lid and simmer until the potatoes are tender and the sauce is slightly thick, 15 to 20 minutes.

Stir in the garam masala. Transfer to a serving dish and garnish with the cilantro.

STUFFED BELL PEPPERS

Bharva Hari Mirch

MAKES 8
SERVINGS (½ STUFFED
PEPPER EACH)

PER SERVING
Calories 40
Carbohydrate 5 g
Fat 2 g
Saturated fat 0 g
Dietary fiber 1.6 g
Protein 1 g
Cholesterol 0 mg
Sodium 275 mg

EXCHANGE
1 vegetable
½ fat

To make any meal look and taste special, serve this very colorful and elegant dish.

> 4 small green bell peppers
>
> 4 teaspoons vegetable oil
>
> ¼ teaspoon brown mustard seeds
>
> 4 cups shredded cabbage
>
> ½ cup grated carrot
>
> ⅛ teaspoon turmeric
>
> 1 teaspoon salt
>
> 1 teaspoon coriander powder
>
> ¼ teaspoon cayenne pepper (optional)

Wash and dry the bell peppers. Cut them in half lengthwise from the stem end. Remove the seeds and cut out the veins, leaving the pepper in a cuplike form. Set aside.

Heat 1 teaspoon of the oil in a large, nonstick frying pan over medium heat. Add the mustard seeds and cover with a lid to avoid splattering. Fry until the mustard seeds stop popping, a few seconds. Add the cabbage and carrot; stir to combine.

Add the turmeric, salt, coriander powder and cayenne pepper (if using); stir to combine. Cover with a lid, and heat through. Reduce the heat and simmer until the vegetables are slightly tender, 5 to 7 minutes. If there is any excess liquid accumulated at the bottom of the pan, increase heat and cook to evaporate it. Remove from the heat and cool to room temperature.

Stuff each bell pepper half with one-eighth of the cabbage mixture.

Clean the frying pan and heat the remaining 3 teaspoons of oil in it over medium heat. Place the stuffed bell peppers in the hot oil with the stuffed side facing up.

Reduce the heat, cover with a lid and simmer until the bell peppers are tender, 10 to 12 minutes. The bottom of the bell peppers will be slightly blackened. Transfer the bell peppers to a platter.

SWEET AND SOUR CARROTS
Gajar ki Subji

MAKES 5
(½-CUP) SERVINGS

PER SERVING
Calories 45
Carbohydrate 9 g
Fat 1 g
Saturated fat 0 g
Dietary fiber 2 g
Protein 1 g
Cholesterol 0 mg
Sodium 255 mg

EXCHANGES
2 vegetables

We love this carrot dish. It tastes a little like glazed carrots, but much more flavorful. This is how it was made at my grandmother's house.

- **1 pound carrots**
- **1 teaspoon vegetable oil**
- **¼ teaspoon cumin seeds**
- **⅛ teaspoon fenugreek seeds**
- **¼ teaspoon turmeric**
- **½ teaspoon salt**
- **2 teaspoons coriander powder**
- **¼ teaspoon cayenne pepper (optional)**
- **¼ cup water**
- **½ teaspoon mango powder**
- **1 tablespoon sugar**

Peel and wash the carrots. Slice into ¼-inch circles. (I often slice carrots in the food processor.) Set aside.

Heat the oil in a heavy skillet over medium-high heat. Add the cumin and fenugreek seeds and fry until the seeds are golden brown, a few seconds.

Add the carrots and stir to combine. Add the turmeric, salt, coriander powder, cayenne pepper (if using), and water. Stir, cover with a lid, reduce the heat and simmer until the carrots are tender, 10 to 12 minutes.

Add the mango powder and sugar and stir to combine. Cook for 3 to 5 minutes. All the liquid from the carrots should be evaporated. If not, increase heat and cook to evaporate it. Transfer to a serving dish.

SPINACH AND POTATOES
Palak Alu

MAKES 4
(½-CUP) SERVINGS

PER SERVING
Calories 55
Carbohydrate 10 g
Fat 1 g
Saturated fat 0 g
Dietary fiber 1.7 g
Protein 2 g
Cholesterol 0 mg
Sodium 321 mg

EXCHANGES
2 vegetables

For this recipe I usually use frozen spinach for convenience; although most stores now carry washed spinach in the salad area. Try it for an extra-special taste.

1 (10-ounce) package frozen chopped spinach

1 medium potato

1 teaspoon vegetable oil

½ teaspoon cumin seeds

½ teaspoon salt

½ teaspoon turmeric

2 teaspoons coriander powder

½ teaspoon cayenne pepper (optional)

Thaw the spinach. Set aside. Peel, wash and cut the potato into 1-inch pieces. Set aside.

Heat the oil in a nonstick skillet over medium heat. Add the cumin seeds and fry until they are golden brown, a few seconds.

Add the potato and spinach and sprinkle with the salt, turmeric, coriander powder and cayenne pepper (if using). Stir to mix. Cover with a lid and heat through. Reduce heat and simmer until the potato is tender, 12 to 15 minutes, stirring once or twice.

If there is any excess liquid, increase the heat and cook to evaporate it. Transfer to a serving dish.

MAKES 4
(½-CUP) SERVINGS

PER SERVING
Calories 80
Carbohydrate 17 g
Fat 2 g
Saturated fat 0 g
Dietary fiber 1.8 g
Protein 1 g
Cholesterol 0 mg
Sodium 403 mg

EXCHANGE
1 starch

SWEET AND SOUR WINTER SQUASH
Kaddu

In my family, this dish was made during festivals and served with puri or kachori (fried breads). Kaddu cooked in this style is my personal favorite vegetable. In India, we always used pumpkin to make this recipe, but a good cooking pumpkin is not always available in the United States. I find butternut squash is an excellent substitution. The fenugreek seeds give this dish a unique flavor

  1 small butternut squash (2 pounds)

  2 teaspoons vegetable oil

  ¼ teaspoon cumin seeds

  ⅛ teaspoon fenugreek seeds

  ½ teaspoon turmeric

  ¾ teaspoon salt

  2 teaspoons coriander powder

  ½ teaspoon cayenne pepper (optional)

  ⅓ cup water

  1 tablespoon fresh lemon juice

  2 tablespoons sugar

Peel and cut the butternut squash in half. Scoop out and discard the inside seeds and threads. Cut into about 1-inch pieces. Rinse, drain and set aside.

In a frying pan, heat the oil over medium-high heat. Add the cumin and fenugreek seeds and cook until the seeds are golden brown, a few seconds.

Add the squash, turmeric, salt, coriander powder, cayenne pepper (if using) and water. Stir to mix. Cover with a lid and bring to a boil. Reduce the heat and simmer until the squash is soft to the touch, 15 to 18 minutes, stirring occasionally.

Add the lemon juice and sugar. Mash the squash with a potato masher or large spoon. Simmer for 5 to 7 minutes, stirring occasionally. Transfer to a serving dish.

MAKES 6
(½-CUP) SERVINGS

PER SERVING
Calories 55
Carbohydrate 6 g
Fat 3 g
Saturated fat 0.4 g
Dietary fiber 1.3 g
Protein 1 g
Cholesterol 0 mg
Sodium 360 mg

EXCHANGES
1 vegetable
½ fat

OKRA WITH TOMATOES
Bhindi Tamatar Ki Subji

Okra is a very popular vegetable in India; it is usually cooked as a dry vegetable. Pick only the tender okra because tough okra does not cook well or absorb any of the spices. I usually add fennel seed powder to my okra recipes to bring out the unique flavor of this vegetable.

1 pound fresh tender okra or frozen whole okra

4 teaspoons vegetable oil

½ teaspoon cumin seeds

1 medium onion, thinly sliced

1 medium tomato, cut in half and sliced into ¼-inch wedges

½ teaspoon turmeric

1 teaspoon salt

1 tablespoon coriander powder

½ teaspoon cayenne pepper (optional)

2 teaspoons fennel seeds, coarsely ground

½ teaspoon mango powder

Wash and drain the okra; pat dry with paper towels. Remove the stem ends and the tips. Slice each okra in half. Set aside. (If using frozen okra, thaw and slice.)

Heat 1 teaspoon of the oil in a nonstick frying pan over medium-high heat. Add the cumin seeds and fry until they turn golden brown, a few seconds.

Add the onion and tomato and layer the okra on top. Sprinkle the turmeric, salt, coriander powder, cayenne pepper (if using) and ground fennel seeds over the okra. Stir gently with a spatula, using a lifting and turning motion.

Cover with a lid, reduce the heat and simmer until the okra is tender, 8 to 10 minutes.

Remove lid, and increase the heat to medium. Add the mango powder and stir gently. Pour the remaining 3 teaspoons oil around the sides of the pan, allowing the oil to flow to the bottom of the pan. Fry for 5 to 7 minutes, stirring gently with a spatula, using a lifting and turning motion.

Transfer to a serving platter.

POTATOES WITH CAULIFLOWER
Alu Gobhi

MAKES 8
(½-CUP) SERVINGS

PER SERVING

Calories 80

Carbohydrate 10 g

Fat 3 g

Saturated fat 0 g

Dietary fiber 1.6 g

Protein 1 g

Cholesterol 0 mg

Sodium 272 mg

EXCHANGE

1 vegetable

½ starch

½ fat

The potato is called the king of vegetables in India. Potatoes are often added to many meat, vegetable and rice dishes. Alu Gobhi is a wonderful combination and it tastes great hot or cold. The cauliflower is often fried to maintain its texture. Here is a lower fat and my personal favorite Alu Gobhi recipe.

1 medium cauliflower

2 medium potatoes

2 tablespoons vegetable oil

Pinch of asafetida (optional)

½ teaspoon cumin seeds

1 small onion, finely chopped

1 teaspoon chopped fresh ginger

¼ teaspoon turmeric

1 teaspoon salt

½ teaspoon cayenne pepper (optional)

2 teaspoons coriander powder

2 teaspoons fresh lemon juice

½ teaspoon Garam Masala (page 48) or purchased

1 tablespoon chopped cilantro (optional)

Trim and divide the cauliflower into 1-inch florets (about 4 cups). Wash and drain well. Set aside.

Peel and wash the potatoes. Cut into 1-inch pieces. Set aside.

Heat 1 tablespoon of the oil in a nonstick skillet over medium-high heat. Add the asafetida (if using) and cumin seeds. Fry until the seeds are golden brown, a few seconds. Add the onion and fry until it is transparent, 3 to 5 minutes, stirring occasionally. Add the cauliflower, potatoes and ginger; stir to combine.

Sprinkle the turmeric, salt and cayenne pepper (if using) over the vegetables. Stir thoroughly to coat the vegetables.

Cover with a lid, heat through and then reduce the heat. Simmer until the vegetables are tender but firm, 8 to 10 minutes.

Sprinkle with the coriander powder, lemon juice and garam masala; stir to combine. Increase the heat to medium and pour the remaining 1 tablespoon of oil around the sides, allowing the oil to flow to the bottom of the pan. Fry for 3 to 5 minutes, stirring occasionally in a lifting and turning fashion to avoid mashing the cauliflower. All the liquid from the vegetables should be evaporated.

Transfer to a serving platter. Garnish with the cilantro, if desired.

MAKES 6
(⅓-CUP) SERVINGS

PER SERVING
Calories 42
Carbohydrate 3 g
Fat 3 g
Saturated fat 0.4 g
Dietary fiber 1 g
Protein 0.5 g
Cholesterol 0 mg
Sodium 358 mg

EXCHANGES
1 vegetable
½ fat

EGGPLANT WITH TOMATOES AND ONIONS

Bengun

Eggplant is cooked in many different ways—by itself or combined with dal, meat or vegetables. When available, use the long Japanese eggplant for this recipe, because it has a mild taste.

1 medium eggplant (¾ pound)

4 teaspoons vegetable oil

¼ teaspoon cumin seeds

¾ cup thinly sliced onion

1 medium tomato, thinly sliced

¼ teaspoon turmeric

½ teaspoon cayenne pepper (optional)

1 teaspoon salt

1 small hot green chile, finely chopped (optional)

2 teaspoons coriander powder

2 teaspoons ground fennel seeds

1 teaspoon fresh lemon juice

Divide the eggplant into quarters, cutting lengthwise and then crosswise. Cut each piece into ¼-inch-thick slices. Set aside.

Heat 1 teaspoon of the oil in a nonstick skillet over medium-high heat. Add the cumin seeds and cook until they are golden brown, a few seconds. Add the onion, tomato and eggplant in that order. Sprinkle the turmeric, cayenne pepper (if using), salt, green chile (if using), coriander powder and fennel seeds over the eggplant.

Stir gently with a spatula in a lifting and turning fashion to coat the vegetables with the spices. Cover with a lid. Cook until the eggplant is soft and somewhat transparent, 10 to 12 minutes, stirring occasionally with a spatula, using a lifting and turning motion.

Remove the lid, sprinkle with the lemon juice and stir. Pour the remaining 3 teaspoons of oil around the sides of the pan, allowing the oil to flow to the bottom, and fry for 5 to 8 minutes, stirring occasionally with a spatula, using a lifting and turning motion. Transfer to a serving dish.

MAKES 8
(½-CUP) SERVINGS

PER SERVING

Calories 38

Carbohydrate 8 g

Fat 0.5 g

Saturated fat 0 g

Dietary fiber 1.7 g

Protein 1 g

Cholesterol 0 mg

Sodium 416 mg

EXCHANGE

1 vegetable

SWEET AND SOUR CABBAGE
Sambhara

The sweet and sour flavor of tamarind sauce gives this vegetable a unique taste. This dish is a specialty of the state of Gujarat. It goes great with any dal or meat. It is often served with Steamed Rice and Bean Cakes (Dhokla, page 67) as a side dish or condiment.

- 1 medium head cabbage (about 2 pounds)
- 2 carrots
- 1 teaspoon vegetable oil
- ½ teaspoon brown mustard seeds
- 6 to 8 curry leaves
- 1 hot green chile, chopped (optional)
- ¼ teaspoon turmeric
- 1½ teaspoons salt
- 2 teaspoons coriander powder
- ½ teaspoon cayenne pepper (optional)
- ½ cup water
- 1 teaspoon tamarind concentrate or 2 tablespoons Tamarind Chutney (page 211)
- 2 tablespoons firmly packed light brown sugar

Remove any tough or discolored cabbage leaves and discard. Cut the cabbage into quarters. Remove the core and slice cabbage into ¼-inch strips. Peel, wash and cut the carrots into thin, matchstick-size strips. Set aside.

Heat the oil in a heavy skillet or wok over medium heat. Add the mustard seeds and curry leaves, cover with a lid to avoid splattering, and cook until the seeds stop popping, a few seconds.

Add the cabbage, carrots and green chile (if using); stir to combine.

Add the turmeric, 1 teaspoon of the salt, coriander powder and cayenne pepper (if using). Stir to coat with the spices. Cover with a lid and heat through. Reduce the heat and cook until the cabbage is transparent and slightly tender, 5 to 6 minutes. Remove from the heat and remove the lid.

To prepare the tamarind sauce, bring the water to a boil in a small saucepan. Add the tamarind concentrate, brown sugar and the remaining ½ teaspoon salt. Reduce the heat and simmer for 5 minutes. If using the chutney, omit the water, brown sugar and ½ teaspoon salt. Add the tamarind sauce or chutney to the cabbage mixture and stir to combine.

Transfer to a serving dish.

PEA AND CHEESE CURRY

Matar Paneer

MAKES 4
(½-CUP) SERVINGS

PER SERVING

Calories 143

Carbohydrate 9 g

Fat 8 g

Saturated fat 3 g

Dietary fiber 2 g

Protein 9 g

Cholesterol 15 mg

Sodium 524 mg

EXCHANGES

1 high-fat meat

½ starch

Matar paneer makes any meal special. Traditionally, the paneer squares were deep-fat fried to a golden brown before adding them to the sauce. I don't fry the paneer and find the taste much more appealing.

1 medium onion, cut into 8 pieces

1 teaspoon chopped fresh ginger

2 tablespoons vegetable oil

½ teaspoon cumin seeds

½ cup tomato sauce

⅓ cup plain nonfat yogurt

¼ teaspoon turmeric

2 teaspoons coriander powder

½ teaspoon cayenne pepper (optional)

3 cups water

2 cups frozen green peas

1 teaspoon salt

1 cup Paneer pieces, made with low-fat milk (page 52)

¾ teaspoon Garam Masala (page 48) or purchased

2 tablespoons chopped cilantro (optional)

In a blender, grind the onion and ginger to a smooth paste. Set aside.

Heat 1 tablespoon of the oil in a nonstick skillet over medium-high heat. Add the cumin seeds and cook until the seeds are golden brown, a few seconds. Add the onion mixture; cook until most of the liquid has evaporated. Add the remaining 1 tablespoon oil and cook until the onion mixture is golden brown, stirring as needed to avoid sticking and burning. Stir in the tomato sauce and continue to cook.

Whip the yogurt with a fork until it is smooth. Gradually add it, 1 tablespoon at a time, to the onion mixture, stirring constantly. Add the turmeric, coriander powder and cayenne pepper (if using). Cook until most of the liquid evaporates and the mixture is thick enough to draw away from the sides and bottom of the pan in a dense mass, stirring occasionally.

Add the water, peas and salt. Bring to a boil, cover with a lid, reduce the heat and simmer for 10 minutes. Add the paneer and simmer for 5 to 7 minutes.

Add the garam masala and stir to combine. Let stand 5 minutes or until ready to serve. Transfer to a serving dish and garnish with the cilantro, if desired.

CABBAGE AND PEAS
Bund Gobhi

MAKES 8
(½-CUP) SERVINGS

PER SERVING

Calories 30

Carbohydrate 4 g

Fat 1 g

Saturated fat 0 g

Dietary fiber 1.5 g

Protein 1 g

Cholesterol 0 mg

Sodium 218 mg

EXCHANGE

1 vegetable

Here is a quick and simple way to cook cabbage. Cabbage can be cooked by itself or with potatoes or peas (as in this recipe). If cooked to the right tenderness (tender but not overcooked), the sweet flavor of cabbage comes through.

> 1 medium head cabbage (about 2 pounds)
>
> 2 teaspoons vegetable oil
>
> ½ teaspoon brown mustard seeds
>
> ½ cup frozen green peas
>
> ¼ teaspoon turmeric
>
> ¾ teaspoon salt
>
> 2 teaspoons coriander powder
>
> ¼ teaspoon cayenne pepper (optional)

Remove any tough or discolored cabbage leaves and discard. Cut the cabbage into quarters. Remove the core and slice the cabbage into ¼-inch strips. Set aside.

Heat the oil in a heavy skillet or wok over medium heat. Add the mustard seeds, cover with a lid to avoid splattering and cook until the seeds stop popping, a few seconds.

Add the cabbage and peas and stir to combine. Add the turmeric, salt, coriander powder and cayenne pepper (if using). Stir to coat with the spices. Cover with a lid and heat through. Reduce the heat and simmer until the cabbage is transparent and slightly tender, 6 to 8 minutes.

Remove the lid, increase the heat and cook until any juices have evaporated, 3 to 5 minutes, stirring occasionally. Transfer to a serving dish.

MAKES 6
(½-CUP) SERVINGS

PER SERVING
Calories 30
Carbohydrate 5 g
Fat 1 g
Saturated fat 0 g
Dietary fiber 1 g
Protein 1 g
Cholesterol 0 mg
Sodium 362 mg

EXCHANGE
1 vegetable

FRENCH-STYLE GREEN BEANS
Bean-Moong ki Subji

For a delicious and simple way to enhance green beans, try them this way. I use frozen French-style green beans.

2 tablespoons moong dal (page 106)

1 teaspoon vegetable oil

½ teaspoon cumin seeds

1 (16-ounce) package frozen French-style green beans

½ teaspoon turmeric

1 teaspoon salt

2 teaspoons coriander powder

¼ teaspoon cayenne pepper (optional)

¾ teaspoon Garam Masala (page 48) or purchased

1 teaspoon fresh lemon juice

Clean the moong dal of any extraneous materials and wash in 3 to 4 changes of water. Set aside.

Heat the oil in a frying pan over medium-high heat. Add the cumin seeds and cook until they are golden brown, a few seconds. Add the green beans and moong dal. Sprinkle with the turmeric and salt and stir to mix. Cover with a lid and heat through. Reduce the heat and simmer until the moong dal mashes easily when 1 or 2 dal are placed on a plate and pressed with your finger, 10 to 12 minutes.

Add the coriander powder, cayenne pepper (if using), garam masala and lemon juice. Stir to coat with the spices. Cook for 2 to 3 minutes to evaporate all the liquid.

Transfer to a serving dish.

SPINACH WITH CHEESE
Palak Paneer

MAKES 8
(½-CUP) SERVINGS

PER SERVING

Calories 122

Carbohydrate 5 g

Fat 7 g

Saturated fat 4 g

Dietary fiber 1.3 g

Protein 11 g

Cholesterol 21 mg

Sodium 492 mg

EXCHANGES

1 high-fat meat

1 vegetable

Whether or not you like spinach, this dish is a must try. For convenience I always use frozen spinach for this recipe. This is another very popular dish in restaurants, where it is typically prepared with cream, making it very high in fat.

1 pound fresh or thawed frozen chopped spinach

1 small onion, cut into 4 pieces

1 teaspoon chopped fresh ginger

1 teaspoon salt

½ teaspoon turmeric

½ teaspoon cayenne pepper (optional)

1 cup water

1½ cups Paneer, made with low-fat milk
  (page 52)

1 teaspoon vegetable oil

½ teaspoon cumin seeds

In a heavy saucepan, mix the spinach, onion, ginger, salt, turmeric, cayenne pepper (if using), and ½ cup of the water. Bring to a boil, reduce the heat, cover with a lid and steam for 5 minutes or until the greens are soft. Set aside to cool.

In a blender, coarsely grind the cooled spinach mixture.

Return the spinach mixture to the pan and stir in the remaining water. Cover with a lid and cook on medium heat until the spinach is simmering. (**Very important:** Before stirring, remove the skillet from the heat and carefully remove the lid and stir. The spinach tends to splatter and can burn.) Reduce the heat and simmer for 20 to 30 minutes; longer cooking time adds flavor to the spinach.

Remove the spinach from the heat, add the paneer and stir. Cover with a lid and return to the heat. Simmer for 8 to 10 minutes. Remove from the heat.

To prepare the chounk (seasoning): In a small frying pan, heat the oil over medium heat, add the cumin seeds and cook until they turn golden brown, a few seconds. Carefully add the chounk to the spinach, stir and cover with a lid. Let stand 5 minutes or until ready to serve.

MAKES 4
(½-CUP) SERVINGS

PER SERVING

Calories 65

Carbohydrate 12 g

Fat 1 g

Saturated fat 0 g

Dietary fiber 2 g

Protein 3 g

Cholesterol 0 mg

Sodium 300 mg

EXCHANGES

1 vegetable

½ starch

FROZEN MIXED VEGETABLES
Sukhi Subji

*When in a hurry, frozen mixed vegetables can be a lifesaver. Great with any meal,
Indian or Western.*

1 teaspoon vegetable oil

¼ teaspoon cumin seeds

1 (16-ounce) package frozen mixed vegetables

¼ teaspoon turmeric

2 teaspoons coriander powder

½ teaspoon salt

¼ teaspoon cayenne pepper (optional)

¼ cup water

1 teaspoon Garam Masala (page 48) or purchased

1 teaspoon fresh lemon juice

Heat the oil in a nonstick skillet over medium-high heat. Add the cumin
seeds and cook until they turn golden brown, a few seconds.

Add the frozen vegetables, turmeric, coriander powder, salt, cayenne pepper (if using) and water. Stir well. Heat through, cover with a lid and simmer until vegetables are tender, 8 to 9 minutes stirring occasionally.

Add the garam masala and lemon juice. If there is any liquid left, increase
heat and cook for a few minutes to evaporate it. Transfer to a serving dish.

MAKES 5
(½-CUP) SERVINGS

PER SERVING
Calories 93
Carbohydrate 13 g
Fat 3 g
Saturated fat 0.4 g
Dietary fiber 3.3 g
Protein 4 g
Cholesterol 0 mg
Sodium 390 mg

EXCHANGES
1 starch
½ fat

SPICY PEAS
Sukhi Matar

I remember shelling fresh peas as a family affair. I now enjoy the convenience of frozen peas. Serve this dish with an Indian or a Western meal.

1 medium onion

1 tablespoon vegetable oil

½ teaspoon cumin seeds

1 (16-ounce) package frozen green peas, thawed

¼ teaspoon turmeric

¼ teaspoon cayenne pepper (optional)

1 tablespoon coriander powder

¾ teaspoon salt

2 tablespoons water

½ teaspoon Garam Masala (page 48) or purchased

Peel and grate onion. Set aside. Heat the oil in a heavy nonstick skillet over medium heat. Add the cumin seeds and cook until they are golden brown, a few seconds.

Add the grated onion and cook, stirring occasionally, until lightly browned.

Add the peas, turmeric, cayenne pepper (if using), coriander powder, salt and water; stir to combine. Cover with a lid and heat through. Reduce the heat and simmer for 10 minutes.

Stir in the garam masala and cook for 3 to 5 minutes, stirring occasionally. If there is any liquid left, increase the heat and cook for a few minutes to evaporate it. Transfer to a serving dish.

MAKES 12
(½-CUP) SERVINGS

PER SERVING
Calories 28
Carbohydrate 4 g
Fat 1 g
Saturated fat 0 g
Dietary fiber 1.7 g
Protein 2 g
Cholesterol 0 mg
Sodium 290 mg

EXCHANGE
1 vegetable

MIXED GREENS
Sag

Sag is a very popular dish from the state of Punjab. It tastes great with wheat or corn roti. Traditionally, it is cooked for hours to blend and to acquire a savory taste, but I use frozen greens and grind them in a blender to get the same taste with much less time and effort.

1 pound mustard greens, cleaned and chopped, or 1 (16-ounce) package frozen chopped mustard greens

10 ounces fresh spinach, cleaned and chopped, or 1 (10-ounce) package frozen chopped spinach

1 small onion, peeled and cut into 8 pieces

1 teaspoon chopped ginger

½ teaspoon turmeric

1½ teaspoons salt

3 cups water

3 tablespoons cornmeal

2 teaspoons vegetable oil

½ teaspoon cumin seeds

2 whole dried red chiles (optional)

½ teaspoon cayenne pepper (optional)

To a heavy saucepan, add the greens, onion, ginger, turmeric, salt and 1 cup of the water. Boil over medium heat for 10 minutes. Set aside to cool.

In a blender, coarsely grind the greens. Grind half of the greens at a time and use the cooking as needed.

Return the pureed greens to the skillet. Add 1½ cups of the water. Cover and bring to a boil. Reduce the heat and simmer, stirring occasionally. (**Very important:** Before stirring, remove the skillet from the heat, and carefully remove the lid and stir. The greens tends to splatter and can burn.)

Mix the cornmeal in the remaining ½ cup of the water. Carefully add to the greens and stir to mix thoroughly. Simmer for 20 minutes. Remove from the heat.

To prepare the chounk (seasoning): Heat the oil in a small frying pan over medium heat. Add the cumin seeds and red chiles (if using) and cook until the seeds are golden brown. Remove from the heat and add the cayenne pepper (if using). With the lid in one hand to prevent spattering, carefully add the chounk to the pureed greens and cover with the lid. Transfer to a serving dish.

MAKES 6
(½-CUP) SERVINGS

POTATO CURRY

Alu Tari

PER SERVING

Calories 70

Carbohydrate 15 g

Fat 1 g

Saturated fat 0 g

Dietary fiber 1 g

Protein 1 g

Cholesterol 0 mg

Sodium 270 mg

EXCHANGE

1 starch

This is a quick-and-easy way to prepare potatoes. It can be made with boiled or raw potatoes. Serve with roti or other bread.

3 medium potatoes, boiled

1 teaspoon vegetable oil

¼ teaspoon cumin seeds

½ teaspoon turmeric

2 teaspoons coriander powder

¼ teaspoon cayenne pepper (optional)

¾ teaspoon salt

2 cups water

½ teaspoon Garam Masala (page 48) or purchased

1 teaspoon fresh lemon juice

1 tablespoon chopped cilantro (optional)

Peel the potatoes and break them into ½- to 1-inch pieces. Set aside.

Heat the oil in a heavy saucepan over medium heat. Add the cumin seeds and cook until the seeds are golden brown, a few seconds.

Add the potatoes and stir to mix. Stir in the turmeric, coriander powder, cayenne pepper (if using), salt and water. Bring to a boil. Reduce the heat to medium, cover partially with a lid and simmer until desired consistency, 12 to 15 minutes.

Add the garam masala and lemon juice and stir to mix. Transfer to a serving dish and garnish with the cilantro, if desired.

CHICKEN

Chicken is the most popular meat served in India. It can be prepared in a simple or elegant manner. The skin is always removed from the chicken before it is cooked. In most Indian dishes the chicken is cut into small parts. The drumsticks and thighs are separated. The breast is cut into four to eight parts. I usually have the butcher skin the chicken and cut it into 2- to 3-inch pieces.

Once the skin is removed, chicken is a very lean choice. I have used both white and dark meat for my recipes, allowing for more flexibility in a family meal. White meat is the leanest of the chicken parts. The dark meat is slightly higher in fat than white meat but still quite lean.

Traditionally, chicken is often marinated in spices, stir-fried in oil, added to the fried spice mixture (*masala*) and cooked or simmered to make the sauce. I have used as little oil as possible to maintain the flavor, texture and taste. The recipes are, therefore, much lower in fat than the traditional recipes but the taste is unaltered.

Enjoy them—from the very lean marinated *Tandoori Murgh* (Barbecued Chicken) to the rich *Mughalai Murgh* (Chicken with Almonds and Raisins). Chicken is usually served with rice or a flat bread. Serve it with salad and/or a vegetable to make an elegant and balanced meal.

For the nutrient analysis I have used approximately half white and half dark meat to give a representative average. However, some recipes do call for white meat only. So for calculating exchanges, the calories may be less than the exchanges that were computed, because lean meat is based on three grams of fat but white meat has only one gram of fat.

MAKES 6 SERVINGS

PER SERVING
Calories 155
Carbohydrate 4 g
Fat 4 g
Saturated fat 1 g
Dietary fiber 0.5 g
Protein 24 g
Cholesterol 66 mg
Sodium 551 mg

EXCHANGES
3 lean meat

BARBECUED CHICKEN
Tandoori Murgh

An elegant dish from the state of Punjab, this is one of the most popular chicken dishes. It is made in a tandoor (clay oven) and hence the name. But it can also be baked in an oven or grilled on a barbecue. It has a deep red color.

3 pounds chicken pieces

1 small onion, peeled

½ cup tomato sauce

½ cup plain nonfat yogurt

1 teaspoon chopped fresh ginger

2 garlic cloves, peeled

2 teaspoons coriander powder

½ teaspoon cayenne pepper (optional)

2 whole cloves

1 teaspoon cumin seeds

4 cardamom pods

1 teaspoon salt

1 teaspoon Garam Masala (page 48) or purchased

¼ teaspoon red food color

Lemon wedges or fresh lemon juice (optional)

Remove the skin and all visible fat from the chicken pieces. Cut 2 or 3 slits, 1 inch long and ½ inch deep, in each piece of chicken. Place in a casserole dish and set aside.

Cut the onion into 4 to 6 pieces. In a blender, put onion, tomato sauce, yogurt, ginger, garlic cloves, coriander powder, cayenne pepper (if using), cloves, cumin seeds, cardamom pods, salt, garam masala and red food color. Blend to a smooth paste.

Pour the tandoori paste over the chicken and turn the pieces to thoroughly coat with the spice mixture. Cover with a lid or plastic wrap and marinate in the refrigerator 4 to 24 hours.

Preheat the oven to 400F (250C). Remove the chicken pieces from the marinade, saving the marinade. Arrange the pieces in a broiler pan. Bake, uncovered, in the middle of the oven for 30 minutes. Turn the pieces over and brush with the remaining marinade. Bake for 10 to 15 minutes until the chicken is tender. (Or cook on a grill over hot coals until chicken is tender, turning often to get a nice red color.)

Turn the oven to broil. Turn the pieces over once again and broil for 5 minutes to get a nice red color.

Transfer the chicken to a serving platter. Serve with lemon wedges or squeeze lemon juice over the chicken before eating, if desired.

CHICKEN CURRY
Murgh Tari

MAKES 6 SERVINGS

PER SERVING

Calories 197

Carbohydrate 4 g

Fat 9 g

Saturated fat 1.8 g

Dietary fiber 0.7 g

Protein 24 g

Cholesterol 67 mg

Sodium 430 mg

EXCHANGES

3½ lean meat

Murgh tari is the most common way to serve chicken. The curry (sauce) tastes great with roti or rice. Typically a large amount of oil is used in preparing the sauce. However, by using a nonstick skillet and all the spices, you can reduce the fat significantly without altering the taste.

3 pounds chicken pieces

2 tablespoons vegetable oil

1 teaspoon cumin powder

4 cardamom pods

2-inch cinnamon stick

1 medium onion, finely chopped

4 garlic cloves, chopped

2 teaspoons chopped fresh ginger

1 medium tomato, finely chopped

½ teaspoon turmeric

1 tablespoons coriander powder

½ teaspoon cayenne pepper (optional)

½ teaspoon fennel seeds, coarsely ground

1 teaspoon coarsely ground black pepper

½ cup plain nonfat yogurt

1 teaspoon salt

½ cup water

2 tablespoons chopped cilantro

1 tablespoon fresh lemon juice

Remove the skin and all visible fat from the chicken pieces. Cut 2 or 3 slits, 1 inch long and ½ inch deep, in each piece of chicken. Set aside.

Heat the oil in a heavy saucepan over medium-high heat. Add the chicken pieces in a single layer and fry until the chicken is white, 3 to 5 minutes, turning the pieces over once or twice. Transfer the chicken to a plate using a slotted spoon.

Add the cumin powder, cardamom pods, cinnamon stick, onion, garlic and ginger to the oil. Fry, stirring constantly, until the onions are golden brown, 7 to 8 minutes.

Stir in the tomato, turmeric, coriander powder, cayenne pepper (if using), fennel seeds and black pepper. Fry for 2 to 3 minutes. Beat yogurt with a wire wisk and add, 1 tablespoon at a time, to the onion marsala, stirring constantly. Fry for 2 to 4 minutes.

Add the chicken and sprinkle with the salt. Stir to coat with the spice mixture. Pour the water evenly over the chicken. Bring to a boil. Reduce the heat to low. Add the cilantro and gently stir the chicken. Cover tightly and simmer until the chicken is tender but does not fall apart, 20 to 25 minutes.

Transfer to a serving platter. Sprinkle with the lemon juice.

MAKES 6 SERVINGS

PER SERVING

Calories 193

Carbohydrate 4 g

Fat 9 g

Saturated fat 1.8 g

Dietary fiber 1 g

Protein 23 g

Cholesterol 67 mg

Sodium 595 mg

EXCHANGES

3 lean meat

1 vegetable

CHICKEN WITH VEGETABLES
Murgh Subji Wala

Served with rice or Naan (page 85), this chicken dish makes a complete and very tasty meal. The vegetables have a starring role and they add color, texture and flavor.

3 pounds chicken pieces

2 tablespoons vegetable oil

1 teaspoon cumin powder

1 medium onion, thinly sliced

2 garlic cloves, chopped

1 teaspoon chopped fresh ginger

1 large bell pepper, sliced into ¼-inch-thick strips

2 medium tomatoes, sliced into ½-inch wedges

¾ cup thinly sliced mushrooms

¼ teaspoon turmeric

¼ teaspoon cayenne pepper (optional)

2 teaspoons coriander powder

1 ½ teaspoons salt

½ teaspoon Garam Masala (page 48) or purchased

Remove the skin and all visible fat from the chicken pieces. Cut 2 or 3 slits, 1 inch long and ½ inch deep, in each piece of chicken. Set aside.

Heat the oil in a heavy saucepan over medium-high heat. Add the chicken pieces in a single layer and fry until the chicken is white, 3 to 5 minutes, turning the pieces over once or twice. Transfer the chicken to a plate using a slotted spoon.

Add the cumin powder, onion, garlic and ginger. Fry, stirring constantly until the onions are golden brown, 7 to 8 minutes.

Add the bell peppers, tomatoes, mushrooms, turmeric, cayenne pepper (if using), coriander powder and salt; stir to combine.

Add the chicken, stirring to mix. Heat through, cover with a lid and reduce the heat. Simmer until the chicken is tender, 20 to 25 minutes.

Remove from the heat and sprinkle with the garam masala. Cover with a lid and let stand 5 minutes or until ready to serve.

CHICKEN IN YOGURT SAUCE
Murgh Khorma

MAKES 6 SERVINGS

PER SERVING

Calories 193

Carbohydrate 3 g

Fat 9 g

Saturated fat 1.8 g

Dietary fiber 0 g

Protein 23 g

Cholesterol 67 mg

Sodium 428 mg

EXCHANGES

3½ lean meat

I often make this when I am in a hurry because it does not need to be marinated—a quick and delicious way to prepare chicken.

3 pounds chicken pieces

½ cup plain nonfat yogurt

1 teaspoon chopped fresh ginger

2 garlic cloves, chopped

2 teaspoons Garam Masala (page 48) or purchased

½ teaspoon cayenne pepper (optional)

1 teaspoon coriander powder

1 teaspoon salt

2 tablespoons vegetable oil

½ teaspoon cumin seeds

1 medium onion, thinly sliced

½ cup water

1 hot green chile, chopped (optional)

2 tablespoons chopped cilantro

Remove the skin and all visible fat from the chicken pieces. Cut into 8 to 10 pieces. Cut 2 or 3 slits, 1 inch long and ½ inch deep, in each piece of chicken. Place in a bowl; set aside.

In a small bowl, mix the yogurt, ginger, garlic, garam masala, cayenne pepper (if using), coriander powder and salt. Pour over the chicken and mix well.

Heat the oil in a heavy saucepan over medium heat. Add the cumin seeds and cook until the seeds are golden brown, a few seconds. Add the onion and fry until it is golden brown, stirring as needed.

Add chicken and the marinade and fry for 8 to 10 minutes. Add the water, green chile (if using) and cilantro and stir well. Cover with a lid and reduce the heat. Simmer until the chicken is tender, 20 to 25 minutes, stirring occasionally. Transfer to a serving dish.

MAKES 6 SERVINGS

PER SERVING

Calories 125

Carbohydrate 0 g

Fat 3 g

Saturated fat 1 g

Dietary fiber 0 g

Protein 22 g

Cholesterol 60 mg

Sodium 408 mg

EXCHANGES

3 lean meat

BLACKENED CHICKEN
Kali Mirch Murgh

This is a quick, low-fat recipe using just white meat. If you like the flavor of black pepper, you will love this dish. It also makes great sandwiches.

> 1 ½ pounds boneless, skinless chicken breasts
>
> 1 teaspoon chopped fresh ginger
>
> 2 garlic cloves, chopped
>
> 1 teaspoon salt
>
> 1 teaspoon coarsely ground black pepper
>
> 1 teaspoon vegetable oil
>
> 1 tablespoon fresh lemon juice

Cut the chicken breast into 1- to 2-inch pieces. (Cut the chicken breast in half for sandwiches.) Rub the chicken pieces with the ginger, garlic, salt and black pepper and set aside.

Heat the oil in a wok or a nonstick skillet over medium-high heat, coating the pan with oil by shaking it. Add the chicken and stir-fry for 10 minutes. Cover with a lid, reduce heat and cook until the chicken is tender, 10 to 12 minutes.

Transfer to a serving platter and sprinkle with the lemon juice.

MAKES 6 SERVINGS

PER SERVING

Calories 241

Carbohydrate 8 g

Fat 11 g

Saturated fat 2 g

Dietary fiber 1 g

Protein 26 g

Cholesterol 67 mg

Sodium 443 mg

EXCHANGES

3 medium-fat meat

½ starch

CHICKEN WITH ALMONDS AND RAISINS

Mughalai Murgh

Chicken fit for a king! The original version is cooked with cream and a large amount of oil, but you will not miss the cream or the fat in this recipe. It is great for parties.

3 pounds chicken pieces

1 large onion, cut into 8 pieces

1-inch piece peeled fresh ginger

4 garlic cloves, peeled

2 tablespoons vegetable oil

1 teaspoon cumin seeds

4 cardamom pods

2 bay leaves

1-inch cinnamon stick

4 whole cloves

1 cup nonfat yogurt

¼ cup water

½ teaspoon cayenne pepper (optional)

1 teaspoon coriander powder

1 teaspoon salt

¼ cup slivered blanched almonds

2 tablespoons golden raisins

½ teaspoon Garam Masala (page 48) or purchased

2 tablespoons chopped cilantro

Remove the skin and all visible fat from the chicken pieces. Cut into 8 to 10 pieces. Cut 2 or 3 slits, 1 inch long and ½ inch deep, in each piece of chicken. Set aside.

In a blender, grind the onion, ginger and garlic. Set aside.

Heat the oil in a heavy saucepan over medium-high heat. Add the chicken pieces in a single layer and fry until the chicken is white, 3 to 5 minutes, turning the pieces over once or twice. Transfer the chicken to a plate using a slotted spoon.

To the same oil, add the cumin seeds, cardamom pods, bay leaves, cinnamon stick and cloves. Fry until the cumin seeds turn golden brown, a few seconds. Add the onion paste and fry until all the liquid evaporates. Beat the yogurt with a fork and gradually add, 1 tablespoon at a time, to the onion masala, stirring constantly until all the yogurt is well blended. Continue to cook until most of the liquid is evaporated and the mixture draws into a dense mass.

Add the chicken and any juices that may have accumulated. Stir thoroughly. Add the water, cayenne pepper (if using), coriander and salt and mix again. Bring to a boil; reduce the heat, cover with a lid and simmer for 20 to 25 minutes.

In the meantime, preheat oven to 300F (150C). Put the almonds in a baking dish and roast them 15 to 20 minutes until light brown, shaking the pan frequently to avoid burning.

Add the raisins to the chicken, stir thoroughly, cover and simmer for 10 minutes. Add 2 tablespoons of the roasted almonds, the garam masala and chopped cilantro and stir gently.

Transfer to a serving platter and garnish with the remaining roasted almonds.

CHICKEN WITH SPINACH
Murgh Sag Wala

PER SERVING

Calories 175

Carbohydrate 6 g

Fat 8 g

Saturated fat 1.5 g

Dietary fiber 2 g

Protein 21 g

Cholesterol 52 mg

Sodium 652 mg

EXCHANGES

3 lean meat

1 vegetable

Served with rice or Naan (page 85), this spinach and chicken dish makes a complete meal. When in a hurry use frozen spinach and buy the chicken already skinned and chopped for an easy-to-fix dish.

2½ pounds chicken parts

1 pound fresh or thawed frozen spinach, chopped

2 tablespoons vegetable oil

1 teaspoon cumin seeds

1 medium onion, finely chopped

1 teaspoon chopped fresh ginger

2 garlic cloves, chopped

½ teaspoon turmeric

½ teaspoon cayenne pepper (optional)

2 teaspoons coriander powder

1½ teaspoons salt

1 teaspoon Garam Masala (page 48) or purchased

2 tablespoons fresh lemon juice

Remove the skin and all visible fat from the chicken pieces. Cut chicken into 2-inch pieces. Set aside.

Chop the fresh spinach or squeeze the thawed frozen spinach lightly between your hands to remove excess water. Set aside.

Heat the oil in a nonstick skillet over medium high heat. Add the chicken pieces in a single layer and fry until chicken is white, 3 to 5 minutes, turning the pieces over once or twice. Transfer the chicken to a plate using a slotted spoon.

To the same oil, add the cumin seeds and cook over medium-high heat until they are golden brown, a few seconds. Add the onion, ginger and garlic. Fry until the onion is lightly brown, stirring occasionally.

Add the spinach and stir to mix. Add the turmeric, cayenne pepper (if using), coriander powder and salt; stir thoroughly.

Add the chicken and stir to combine. Cover with a lid, heat through and reduce the heat. Simmer for 20 to 25 minutes, stirring occasionally. Remove the lid and increase the heat to evaporate any excess liquid.

Remove from the heat and sprinkle with the garam masala and lemon juice. Cover with a lid and let stand 5 minutes or until ready to serve.

STIR-FRIED CHICKEN
Mysore Murgh

MAKES 6 SERVINGS

PER SERVING

Calories 162

Carbohydrate 2 g

Fat 7 g

Saturated fat 1.5 g

Dietary fiber 0 g

Protein 23 g

Cholesterol 66 mg

Sodium 414 mg

EXCHANGES

3 lean meat

As the name indicates, this dish is from the state of Mysore. The seasonings of urad dal and fennel seeds give this dish a unique flavor. The bones are usually not removed, because they add flavor to the dish. If you choose, you can use boneless chicken breasts for this recipe, and the fat content will then be lower. If using boneless, skinless chicken breasts, substitute 1½ pounds for the 3 pounds of chicken pieces.

3 pounds chicken pieces

1 teaspoon salt

¼ teaspoon turmeric

1 tablespoon vegetable oil

½ teaspoon brown mustard seeds

½ teaspoon urad dal (page 106)

½ teaspoon fennel seeds

3 whole dried red chiles

1 large onion, finely chopped

3 tablespoons water

Onion and Tomato Salad (page 201; optional)

Remove the skin and all visible fat from the chicken pieces. Cut chicken into 2-inch pieces. Rub salt and turmeric on the chicken pieces. Set aside.

Heat the oil in a wok or a frying pan over medium-high heat. Add the mustard seeds, cover with a lid to avoid splattering and cook until they stop popping, a few seconds. Add the dal, fennel seeds and red chiles. Fry until the chiles darken, a few seconds. Add the onion and fry until light brown, stirring occasionally.

Add the chicken and fry for about 5 minutes, stirring constantly. Add the water, about 1 tablespoon at a time, while continuing to stir. Cook until the chicken is tender and slightly brown, 10 to 12 minutes.

Transfer to a serving platter and garnish with the salad, if desired.

PER SERVING

Calories 176

Carbohydrate 5 g

Fat 7 g

Saturated fat 1.5 g

Dietary fiber 1.4 g

Protein 23 g

Cholesterol 66 mg

Sodium 418 mg

EXCHANGES

3 lean meat

1 vegetable

CORIANDER CHICKEN
Dhania Murgh

The cilantro (coriander) leaves give this dish a fresh flavor. Combined with tomatoes and green bell pepper, it makes a very colorful and tasty dish.

1½ pounds boneless, skinless chicken breasts

1 teaspoon salt

1-inch piece peeled fresh ginger

2 garlic cloves, peeled

1 medium onion, cut into 6 to 8 pieces

1 cup cilantro leaves

1 hot green chile (optional)

2 medium tomatoes

2 medium green bell peppers

2 tablespoons vegetable oil

Cut the chicken into 2-inch pieces. Season with the salt; set aside.

In a blender, grind the ginger, garlic, onion, cilantro and green chile (if using) to a smooth paste. Add to chicken and marinate for 20 to 30 minutes at room temperature.

Cut the tomatoes and bell peppers into 1-inch pieces; set aside.

Coat a wok or a skillet with the oil and heat over medium-high heat. Add the chicken with the marinade and stir-fry for 8 to 10 minutes, stirring constantly. Add the tomatoes and bell peppers and stir to combine. Cover with a lid and simmer for 10 minutes. Transfer to a serving dish.

FISH AND SHRIMP

In India the states of Bengal and Kerala are known for their fish dishes. The important thing to remember about fish is the fresher the fish, the better the taste. Make sure the fish you buy is fresh. It should be shiny with good color, firm to the touch and mild and fresh in aroma. Do not buy dull or faded fish or ones that have a pronounced "fishy" smell. If fresh fish is not available, frozen fish can be used. Never overcook fish.

Fish is often breaded, fried and/or curried for Indian dishes. Breaded and fried fish are not included in this book. A minimum amount of oil is used in preparation and the fat content is kept very low without compromising any of the taste.

Flounder, cod, halibut, orange roughy and perch work well for Indian dishes. These varieties are naturally low in fat and calories so you can enjoy trying the tasty recipes given here.

For the nutritional analysis, cod has been used. For calculating the exchanges, the calories may be less than the exchanges state, because lean meat is based on three grams of fat and fish has about one gram of fat per ounce.

MAKES 6 SERVINGS

PER SERVING

Calories 155

Carbohydrate 3 g

Fat 6 g

Saturated fat 0.8 g

Dietary fiber 0 g

Protein 22 g

Cholesterol 45 mg

Sodium 432 mg

EXCHANGES

3 lean meat

FISH CURRY
Machhi Tari

Meat or vegetables in a sauce (curry) is a very popular way to prepare food. The curry tastes good with rice or roti. This is a lightly seasoned fish in a sauce. Choose a fish of your liking.

1 ½ pounds fish fillets

½ teaspoon turmeric

¼ teaspoon cayenne pepper (optional)

1 teaspoon salt

1 medium onion, cut into 8 pieces

1-inch piece peeled fresh ginger

2 garlic cloves, peeled

2 tablespoons vegetable oil

1 large tomato, chopped

½ teaspoon cumin powder

1 teaspoon coriander powder

¼ cup plain nonfat yogurt

1 cup water

2 tablespoons chopped cilantro (optional)

Cut the fish into 3- to 4-inch pieces. Place the fish in a bowl and sprinkle with the turmeric, cayenne pepper (if using) and salt, turning to coat well. Set aside.

In a blender, grind the onion, ginger and garlic to a paste. Set aside.

Heat 1 tablespoon of the oil in a nonstick skillet over medium-high heat. Add the fish in a single layer and cook for 1 minute on each side. Remove with a slotted spoon and set aside.

Add the onion paste to the skillet and cook until most of the liquid is evaporated, stirring occasionally. Add the remaining 1 tablespoon oil and fry until the onion is light brown.

Reduce the heat to medium. Add the tomatoes, cumin powder and corian-der powder. Fry for 3 to 5 minutes. Beat the yogurt lightly with a fork and add, 1 tablespoon at a time, to the onion mixture, stirring constantly. Cook until most of the liquid is evaporated and the onion masala draws into a dense mass.

Add the fish pieces, stirring gently to coat with the spice mixture. Pour the water evenly over the fish. Bring to a boil. Reduce the heat to low. Cover tightly and simmer for 5 to 7 minutes.

Transfer to a serving platter. Sprinkle with the cilantro, if desired.

BAKED FISH WITH BLACK PEPPER

Machhi Kali Mirch

Here the fish is marinated and baked with garlic and herbs. If desired, marinate the fish the night before and refrigerate it. You can either bake it or stir-fry it in a pan.

2 pounds fish fillets

1 teaspoon salt

¼ teaspoon turmeric

1 teaspoon cumin powder

1 teaspoon black pepper

2 garlic cloves, chopped

2 teaspoons vegetable oil

1 tablespoon fresh lemon juice

Place the fish in a bowl, sprinkle with the salt, turmeric, cumin powder, black pepper and garlic, turning to coat well. Cover and marinate for 20 minutes at room temperature or longer in the refrigerator.

Preheat the oven to 400F (205C). Coat the bottom of a baking dish with the oil. Place the fish in a single layer and pour the marinade over it. Bake, uncovered, for 20 to 25 minutes or until the fish is firm to the touch and easily flakes with a fork. Sprinkle with lemon juice.

MAKES 8 SERVINGS

PER SERVING

Calories *119*

Carbohydrate *0 g*

Fat *2.5 g*

Saturated fat *0.5 g*

Dietary fiber *0 g*

Protein *22 g*

Cholesterol *40 mg*

Sodium *315 mg*

EXCHANGES

3 lean meat

MAKES 6 SERVINGS

PER SERVING
Calories 148
Carbohydrate 4 g
Fat 4 g
Saturated fat 0.6 g
Dietary fiber 1.5 g
Protein 23 g
Cholesterol 40 mg
Sodium 409 mg

EXCHANGES
3 lean meat
1 vegetable

FISH WITH BOTTLE GOURD
Machhi aur Lauki

Fish is often cooked with a variety of vegetables for a change of flavor and taste. I use bottle gourd or zucchini, depending on the availability or my mood.

1 ½ pounds fish fillets

1 teaspoon cumin powder

2 garlic cloves, chopped

1 teaspoon chopped fresh ginger

½ teaspoon cayenne pepper (optional)

½ teaspoon turmeric

1 pound bottle gourd or zucchini

3 medium firm tomatoes or 1 cup chopped canned tomatoes, drained

1 tablespoon vegetable oil

1 teaspoon salt

1 tablespoon chopped cilantro

1 tablespoon fresh lemon juice

Place the fish in a bowl. Sprinkle with the cumin powder, garlic, ginger, cayenne pepper, (if using) and turmeric. Set aside. Cut the bottle gourd and tomatoes into 1-inch squares. Set aside.

Heat the oil in a heavy nonstick skillet over medium heat. Add the fish and fry on each side for 1 to 2 minutes.

Add the bottle gourd and tomatoes, sprinkle with the salt and stir with a lifting motion to blend in the spices. Bring to a boil, cover with a lid and simmer for 4 to 5 minutes. Remove the lid, add the cilantro and lemon juice and stir gently. Increase the heat to evaporate any excess liquid and cover until the sauce thickens and clings to the fish and vegetables.

Transfer to a serving platter.

FISH IN MUSTARD SAUCE
Sarson Wali Machhi

MAKES 6 SERVINGS

PER SERVING

Calories 139

Carbohydrate 2 g

Fat 3 g

Saturated fat 0.4 g

Dietary fiber 0 g

Protein 24 g

Cholesterol 40 mg

Sodium 404 mg

EXCHANGES

3 lean meat

The state of Bengal is famous for its fish, which is generally prepared in mustard oil. This is a simple dish that can be marinated ahead of time and microwaved or baked when ready to serve.

> 1 ½ pounds fish fillets
>
> 1 teaspoon salt
>
> ½ teaspoon turmeric
>
> ¼ cup brown mustard seeds
>
> ¾ cup water

Place the fish in a microwave-safe container in a single layer. Sprinkle ½ teaspoon of the salt and ¼ teaspoon of the turmeric on the fish and rub in. Set aside.

Grind the mustard seeds and the remaining salt and turmeric with water the to a fine paste.

Pour the mustard paste on the fish, covering both sides. Cover with plastic wrap. Marinate for 20 minutes at room temperature or longer in the refrigerator (it can be marinated overnight).

Microwave on HIGH for 5 minutes, turn the dish 90 degrees and microwave for 4 to 7 minutes longer. Fish should be firm to the touch and flake easily when probed with a fork.

PER SERVING

Calories 65

Carbohydrate 3 g

Fat 0.5 g

Saturated fat 0.2 g

Dietary fiber 0 g

Protein 11 g

Cholesterol 83 mg

Sodium 394 mg

EXCHANGES

1½ lean meat

BARBECUED SHRIMP

Tandoori Jhinga

This dish, popular with both adults and children, adds a special touch to any barbecue party. It is made in a tandoor (clay oven) and hence the name. But it can also be baked in an oven or grilled on a barbecue.

1 pound medium or large shrimp

¾ cup plain nonfat yogurt

1 teaspoon finely chopped garlic

1 teaspoon grated fresh ginger

1 teaspoon Garam Masala (page 48) or purchased

½ teaspoon salt

1 teaspoon freshly ground black pepper

1 teaspoon red food color (optional)

Shell and devein the shrimp, leaving the tails on. Butterfly them by slicing lengthwise from the head to the tail, leaving the tails intact. Set aside.

In a medium glass bowl, mix the yogurt, garlic, ginger, garam masala, salt, black pepper and food color (if using). Blend thoroughly. Add the shrimp and marinate for 2 to 6 hours in the refrigerator.

Preheat a grill or broiler. Lightly oil 6 metal skewers.

Thread 5 or 6 shrimps on each oiled skewer. Grill or broil for 5 to 7 minutes on each side, until lightly blackened. Serve directly on skewers or remove from skewers and place on a bed of rice or lettuce.

SHRIMP IN YOGURT SAUCE

Jhinga Tari

Spicy yogurt sauce adds a nice creamy taste and texture to the shrimp. It is great for special occasions or anytime you want to impress your guests.

1 ½ pounds shrimp, shelled and deveined

¾ teaspoon salt

2 tablespoons vegetable oil

1 medium onion, finely chopped

2 garlic cloves, chopped

1 teaspoon chopped fresh ginger

½ teaspoon cumin powder

¼ teaspoon turmeric

¼ teaspoon cayenne pepper (optional)

1 teaspoon coriander powder

¼ cup plain nonfat yogurt

½ cup water

½ teaspoon Garam Masala (page 48) or purchased

1 teaspoon fresh lemon juice

1 tablespoon chopped cilantro

Season the shrimp with ¼ teaspoon of the salt and set aside. Heat the oil in a nonstick skillet over medium-high heat. Add the onion, garlic and ginger. Fry until the onion is golden brown, stirring constantly.

Reduce the heat to medium. Add the turmeric, cayenne pepper (if using) and coriander powder. Lightly beat the yogurt with a fork and add, 1 table-spoon at a time, to the onion mixture, stirring constantly. Cook until all the yogurt is absorbed and the mixture forms a thick mass.

Add the shrimp and the remaining ½ teaspoon salt, stirring to coat with the spice mixture. Pour the water evenly over the shrimp. Bring to a boil. Reduce the heat to low, cover tightly and simmer until the shrimp are firm to the touch, 8 to 10 minutes. Sprinkle with the garam masala and stir lightly.

Transfer to a serving platter. Sprinkle with the lemon juice and garnish with cilantro.

SHRIMP WITH TOMATOES

Tamatari Jhinga

MAKES 6
(½-CUP) SERVINGS

PER SERVING
Calories 107
Carbohydrate 9 g
Fat 5 g
Saturated fat 0.7 g
Dietary fiber 2 g
Protein 7 g
Cholesterol 55 mg
Sodium 430 mg

EXCHANGES
1 medium-fat meat
1 vegetable

If you are in a hurry, buy frozen, deveined shrimp and use canned tomatoes. The sweet and sour taste often makes this a favorite of children.

1 pound jumbo shrimp

2 tablespoons fresh lemon juice

1 teaspoon ground cumin

¼ teaspoon turmeric

¼ teaspoon cayenne pepper

¼ teaspoon coarsely ground black pepper

1 teaspoon salt

2 tablespoons vegetable oil

½ teaspoon brown mustard seeds

1 medium onion, finely chopped

1 teaspoon chopped fresh ginger

2 garlic cloves, finely chopped

6 medium firm tomatoes, cut into 1-inch squares or 2 cups
    chopped canned tomatoes, drained

1 tablespoon jaggery (page 38) or brown sugar

2 tablespoons chopped cilantro

Shell and devein the shrimp. Wash and pat dry. In a medium bowl, combine the lemon juice, ground cumin, turmeric, cayenne pepper, black pepper and ½ teaspoon of the salt. Mix well with a fork. Add the shrimp and toss well. Cover and set aside.

Heat the oil in heavy skillet over medium heat. Add the mustard seeds, cover with a lid to avoid splattering and cook until the seeds stop popping, a few seconds. Add the onion, ginger and garlic. Fry until the onion is golden brown.

Drain the marinade into the skillet (don't add the shrimp yet). Add the tomatoes and cook for 3 to 5 minutes. Add the remaining salt and jaggery or brown sugar and stir to combine.

Add the shrimp and cook until it is transparent and firm to the touch, 3 to 5 minutes. Add the cilantro and transfer to a serving platter.

MEAT

I have chosen to include only lamb recipes in this chapter. If desired, however, most of the lamb recipes can be substituted with beef and some with pork. Hindus typically do not eat beef and Muslims do not eat pork.

Lamb can be very high in fat. To reduce the fat, use the leg of lamb for most of the dishes. Trim all the fat and chop or grind the meat. Lamb, beef or pork can all be easily incorporated into a healthy low-fat meal plan. The key is to select lean cuts, trim all visible fat and prepare them with low-fat cooking methods. In India, bones are left in most of the lamb dishes because bones enhance the flavor of the sauce (curry). However, I find boneless lamb much easier to cook and serve. For convenience, I almost always have the butcher trim and chop or grind the meat to my specifications.

Traditionally, lamb is first roasted in oil (*bhuna*) before it is added to the fried spice mixture (*masala*) and cooked or simmered to make the sauce (curry). A fair amount of oil may be floating on top of the curry. I have used as little oil as possible to maintain the *bhuna* flavor, texture and taste. The recipes here are much lower in fat than the traditional ones. Meat is often cooked with vegetables. The vegetables not only act as a meat extender but also add their own unique flavors to the sauce. Plus they absorb the flavor of the meat and together they make a great combination.

For the nutritional analysis, trimmed leg of lamb was used. The exchanges have been computed to the closest calories possible.

CHOPPED SPICY LAMB

Gosht Kalia

MAKES 8 SERVINGS

PER SERVING

Calories 197

Carbohydrate 2 g

Fat 10 g

Saturated fat 2.7 g

Dietary fiber 0.5 g

Protein 23 g

Cholesterol 70 mg

Sodium 320 mg

EXCHANGES

3 medium-fat meat

Gosht Kalia makes any dinner an elegant event. The roasted almonds add extra crunch and give the dish a festive look. Substitute lean chopped beef or pork, if desired.

1 large onion, finely chopped

1 garlic clove, chopped

1 tablespoon chopped fresh ginger

1 hot green chile, chopped (optional)

2 pounds lean boneless lamb, cut into 1-inch cubes

2 tablespoons vegetable oil

4 whole cloves

4 cardamom pods

2-inch cinnamon stick

1 teaspoon cumin powder

1 tablespoon coriander powder

1 teaspoon salt

⅓ cup water

2 tablespoons fresh lemon juice

2 tablespoons roasted slivered almonds

In a blender, grind the onion, garlic, ginger and green chile (if using). Set aside.

In a heavy, ungreased skillet, cook the lamb over medium-high heat until it turns brown. Transfer the lamb to a bowl and set aside, discarding any fat in the skillet.

In the same skillet, heat the oil. Add the cloves, cardamom pods, cinnamon stick, cumin powder and coriander powder and cook for a few seconds. Add the onion mixture and cook until light brown, stirring occasionally.

Add the lamb and salt, stirring to coat with the spices. Add the water, stir and bring to a boil. Cover, reduce the heat and simmer until the lamb is tender, 20 to 30 minutes.

The sauce should be fairly thick. If there is excess liquid, increase the heat and cook to evaporate it. Remove from the heat.

Add the lemon juice and stir to combine. Transfer to a serving dish and garnish with the almonds before serving.

MAKES 6 SERVINGS

PER SERVING

Calories 187

Carbohydrate 4 g

Fat 8 g

Saturated fat 2.4 g

Dietary fiber 1 g

Protein 23 g

Cholesterol 67 mg

Sodium 425 mg

EXCHANGES

3 lean meat

1 vegetable

GROUND LAMB WITH PEAS
Kheema

This is one of the most common ways to serve lamb. It tastes great served hot or cold. Substitute lean ground beef if desired. Ground lamb is often very high in fat; for leaner meat have the butcher grind a trimmed leg of lamb.

1 ½ pounds lean ground lamb

1 tablespoon vegetable oil

1 medium onion, finely chopped

4 garlic cloves, chopped

1 teaspoon chopped fresh ginger

1 teaspoon cumin powder

1 teaspoon coriander powder

¼ teaspoon cayenne pepper (optional)

1 hot green chile, finely chopped (optional)

1 ¼ cups water

¾ cup fresh or frozen green peas

4 tablespoons chopped cilantro

1 teaspoon salt

1 teaspoon Garam Masala (page 48) or purchased

1 tablespoon fresh lemon juice

Heat a heavy skillet over medium heat, add the lamb and cook until brown, stirring to break up. With a slotted spoon take out the lamb and set aside, discarding any fat.

In the same skillet, heat the oil. Add the onion, garlic and ginger and cook until the onion is light brown, stirring occasionally.

Add the lamb, cumin powder, coriander powder, cayenne pepper (if using) and green chile (if using). Stir to combine.

Add ¾ cup of the water and bring to a boil. Cover, reduce the heat and simmer for 20 minutes, stirring occasionally.

Add the peas, 2 tablespoons of the cilantro, the salt, garam masala, lemon juice and the remaining ½ cup water. Stir and simmer covered for 15 minutes. All the liquid should be absorbed, but if not, remove the lid and cook for another few minutes to evaporate it.

Transfer to a serving dish and garnish with the remaining cilantro.

CHOPPED LAMB
Madrasi Gosht

MAKES 8 SERVINGS

PER SERVING

Calories 185

Carbohydrate 1 g

Fat 9 g

Saturated fat 2.5 g

Dietary fiber 0 g

Protein 22 g

Cholesterol 69 mg

Sodium 320 mg

EXCHANGES

3 lean meat

As the name suggests this is from the state of Madras. The mustard seeds and the curry leaves lend a very distinct flavor to this dish. You may substitute lean chopped beef or pork, if desired.

2 pounds lean boneless lamb, cut into ½-inch pieces

1 teaspoon salt

2 teaspoons coriander powder

1 teaspoon cumin powder

¼ teaspoon cayenne pepper (optional)

2 teaspoons freshly ground black pepper

2 tablespoons vegetable oil

1 teaspoon brown mustard seeds

10 curry leaves

1 large onion, thinly sliced

1 teaspoon chopped fresh ginger

1½ cups water

1 tablespoon fresh lemon juice

2 tablespoons chopped cilantro (optional)

In a large bowl, place the lamb and sprinkle with the salt, coriander powder, cumin powder, cayenne pepper (if using) and black pepper. Stir well to coat with the spices. Let stand at room temperature for about 30 minutes.

Heat the oil in a heavy skillet over medium heat. Add the mustard seeds and cover with a lid to avoid splattering. Add the curry leaves, onion and ginger. Cook until the onion is light brown, stirring occasionally.

Add the lamb and its marinade and cook, stirring for about 5 minutes, mixing in all the spices and onion. Stir in the water and bring to a boil. Cover with a lid, reduce the heat and simmer undisturbed for 30 to 45 minutes. The lamb should be tender when pierced with a knife.

The sauce should be thick; if necessary, increase the heat and continue to cook until the sauce thickens.

Sprinkle with the lemon juice and cilantro, if desired. Stir gently. Serve immediately or cover and let stand until ready to serve. Transfer to a serving platter and serve hot.

BARBECUED LAMB ON SKEWERS
Seekh Kebabs

MAKES 6 SKEWERS

PER SKEWER

Calories 135

Carbohydrate 1 g

Fat 7 g

Saturated fat 2 g

Dietary fiber 0 g

Protein 16 g

Cholesterol 50 mg

Sodium 306 mg

EXCHANGES

2 medium-fat meat

Seekh (skewer) kebabs are usually barbecued on a grill, but they can be baked in the oven. Served with Cilantro Chutney (page 209), they can be eaten as an appetizer or part of a meal. Substitute lean beef, if desired.

1 medium onion, cut into 6 to 8 pieces

1-inch piece peeled fresh ginger

2 garlic cloves, peeled

1 teaspoon salt

¼ teaspoon cayenne pepper (optional)

½ teaspoon coriander powder

½ teaspoon cumin powder

¾ teaspoon Garam Masala (page 48) or purchased

1 pound lean ground lamb

In a blender, grind the onion, ginger and garlic. Mix in the salt, cayenne pepper (if using), coriander powder, cumin powder and garam masala.

In a bowl, mix the lamb and onion mixture thoroughly. Let stand for 20 to 30 minutes.

Preheat broiler or grill.

Divide the lamb mixture into 6 equal portions. Lightly oil 6 metal skewers. Shape the lamb mixture into sausage shapes on the lightly oiled skewers, about 1 inch thick, gently pressing all around.

Broil or grill for 10 to 12 minutes on each side, or until well done.

LAMB IN YOGURT SAUCE
Rogan Josh

MAKES 6 SERVINGS

PER SERVING

Calories 175

Carbohydrate 3 g

Fat 6 g

Saturated fat 2.3 g

Dietary fiber 0 g

Protein 25 g

Cholesterol 72 mg

Sodium 439 mg

EXCHANGES

3 lean meat

This dish originates from the state of Kashmir. It does not use any onions or garlic and has a well-blended flavor. The paprika adds a red color; increase the amount if you want to enhance the color.

1 cup plain nonfat yogurt

2 teaspoons chopped fresh ginger

½ teaspoon freshly ground black pepper

½ teaspoon turmeric

½ teaspoon cayenne pepper (optional)

1 teaspoon salt

1½ pounds lean boneless lamb, cut into 1-inch pieces

1 cup water

2 tablespoons chopped cilantro

1 teaspoon paprika

½ teaspoon Garam Masala (page 48) or purchased

Pinch of ground nutmeg

In a large bowl, combine the yogurt, ginger, black pepper, turmeric, cayenne pepper (if using) and salt, mixing well. Add the lamb, turning the pieces with a large spoon to coat with the spices. Cover and marinate at room temperature for about 1 hour or in the refrigerator for 2 hours or more.

Place the lamb and its marinade in a heavy skillet and cook over high heat. Bring to a boil, stirring constantly. Reduce the heat to low, cover the skillet tightly and simmer undisturbed for 30 to 40 minutes.

Pour the water down the sides of the pan and sprinkle with the cilantro and paprika. Stir gently. Cover and simmer until the lamb is tender, 15 to 30 minutes. Cover and let stand 5 minutes or until ready to serve.

Transfer to a serving platter and sprinkle the top with garam masala and nutmeg before serving.

MAKES 6 SERVINGS

PER SERVING

Calories 172

Carbohydrate 4 g

Fat 10 g

Saturated fat 2.3 g

Dietary fiber 0 g

Protein 17 g

Cholesterol 82 mg

Sodium 416 mg

EXCHANGES

2½ medium-fat meat

LAMB MEATBALLS

Koftas

Koftas are made with a variety of meats and vegetables. They are usually deep-fat fried and then cooked in a sauce. I usually bake mine and then add them to a low-fat sauce. For best results, cook this dish a few hours before serving so that the meatballs will absorb the flavor of the sauce. Substitute lean ground beef, if desired.

1 pound lean ground lamb

1 egg

1 teaspoon salt

2 medium onions, cut into 6 to 8 pieces

1 inch chopped fresh ginger

4 garlic cloves

1 hot green chile (optional)

2 tablespoons vegetable oil

½ teaspoon cumin seeds

½-inch cinnamon stick

½ cup plain nonfat yogurt

½ teaspoon turmeric

1 teaspoon coriander powder

1 teaspoon freshly ground black pepper

1½ cup water

1½ teaspoons Garam Masala (page 48) or purchased

Preheat oven to 450F (230C).

In a bowl, put the lamb, egg and ½ teaspoon of the salt and mix well. Wetting your hands with cold water to keep the meat from sticking, make about 1½-inch balls, packing firmly.

Place the meatballs in a single layer in a lightly oiled baking dish. Bake for 18 to 20 minutes, until meat is no longer pink.

Remove from the oven, discarding any fat and transfer the meatballs to a shallow baking dish with a slotted spoon. Reduce the oven to 300F (150C).

In the meantime, grind the onions, ginger, garlic and green chile (if using) in a blender. Set aside.

Heat the oil in a heavy skillet over medium heat. Add the cumin seeds and cinnamon stick. Fry until the cumin seeds are golden brown, a few seconds. Add the onion paste. Fry until light brown, stirring occasionally.

Beat the yogurt with a wire wisk and add, 1 tablespoon at a time, to the onion mixture, stirring constantly. Add the turmeric, coriander powder, black pepper and the remaining ½ teaspoon of salt. Fry until the mixture is thick and draws into a dense mass, stirring occasionally. Add the water and bring to a boil, reduce the heat and simmer for 5 minutes.

Pour the sauce over the meatballs and sprinkle with the garam masala. Cover with aluminum foil and bake at 300F (150C) for 15 to 20 minutes. Serve immediately or cover and let stand until ready to serve.

LAMB WITH POTATOES
Alu Gosht

MAKES 6 SERVINGS

PER SERVING

Calories 244

Carbohydrate 18 g

Fat 8 g

Saturated fat 2.4 g

Dietary fiber 2 g

Protein 23 g

Cholesterol 67 mg

Sodium 594 mg

EXCHANGES

3 lean meat

1 starch

In India meat is often combined with potatoes. The potatoes absorb the flavor of the meat and the two taste great together. Serve with rice and salad for a complete meal. Substitute lean chopped beef or pork, if desired.

1 ½ pounds lean boneless lamb, cut into 1-inch pieces

1 tablespoon vegetable oil

1 medium onion, thinly sliced

2 garlic cloves, chopped

1 tablespoon chopped fresh ginger

1 teaspoon cumin powder

½ teaspoon turmeric

½ teaspoon cayenne pepper (optional)

3 medium tomatoes, cut into 1-inch pieces or 1 (16-ounce) can chopped tomatoes

3 medium potatoes, peeled and cut into 1 ½-inch pieces

1 ½ teaspoons salt

3 cups water

2 tablespoons chopped cilantro

In a heavy skillet, cook the lamb until it turns brown. Transfer the lamb to a bowl and set aside. Discard any fat in the skillet.

Heat the oil in the same skillet over medium-high heat. Add the onion, garlic and ginger. Fry until the onion is light brown, stirring occasionally. Add the lamb, cumin powder, turmeric and cayenne pepper (if using).

Add the tomatoes, potatoes and salt. Cook, stirring, for 5 minutes, completely blending in all the spices. Add the water and bring to a boil. Cover with a lid, reduce the heat and simmer undisturbed for 30 to 45 minutes until the meat is tender.

Sprinkle with the cilantro and stir. The sauce should be thick; if necessary, increase the heat and cook to the desired consistency.

PER SERVING:

Calories 107

Carbohydrate 1 g

Fat 4 g

Saturated fat 1.4 g

Dietary fiber 0 g

Protein 15 g

Cholesterol 46 mg

Sodium 311 mg

EXCHANGES

2 lean meat

LAMB KEBABS

Boti Kebabs

Lamb kebabs are very popular and help make any party a great success. The marinated lamb can be barbecued on the grill or baked in the oven. Substitute lean chopped beef, if desired.

> 1 pound lean boneless lamb, cut into 1- to 2-inch cubes
>
> ⅓ cup plain nonfat yogurt
>
> 1 tablespoon chopped fresh ginger
>
> 2 garlic cloves, chopped
>
> ¼ teaspoon cayenne pepper
>
> 1 teaspoon coriander powder
>
> ¾ teaspoon salt
>
> ½ teaspoon Garam Masala (page 48) or purchased

Cook lamb in a heavy dry skillet over low heat for 10 to 15 minutes. Discard any juices. Pat dry with paper towels and place in a mixing bowl.

Mix the yogurt, ginger, garlic, cayenne pepper, coriander powder, salt and garam masala in a small bowl. Add to the lamb and stir to coat with the spices. Marinate for 2 hours at room temperature or overnight in the refrigerator.

Preheat the broiler or grill. Lightly oil 6 metal skewers.

Thread 5 or 6 lamb pieces on each oiled skewer, leaving a little gap between each piece. Brush with the marinade.

Broil or grill the lamb skewers for 10 minutes on each side, until tender. Brush with the remaining marinade to prevent drying. Do not overcook. Serve hot.

YOGURT, SALADS
AND CHUTNEYS

Yogurt is an essential part of many Indian meals. Plain yogurt is eaten all over India. It is served plain or as *raita*, which is yogurt combined with variety of vegetables or occasionally with sugar and fruit. Yogurt is mostly eaten with a dash of salt, which is such a great contrast to the sweetened yogurt eaten in the Western world. Plain yogurt often accompanies a meal as a side dish; it is soothing and cooling with a spicy meal. In south India, a meal is invariably topped off with rice and plain yogurt.

Nutritionally speaking, yogurt combined with grains also provides the amino acids to make complete protein.

Salads are often served with a meal to add crunch and variety. Favorite ingredients are cucumbers, tomatoes, onions and radishes. Lettuce is not as popular in India as in the Western world, although it is catching on. Salads are more often served as a relish than as a meal or a side dish.

Chutneys and pickles are condiments that are served with meals. They come in salty, sour, sweet and hot flavors. The pickles are very potent and only a dab is needed to perk up any meal. Pickles are usually made in huge jars and kept for one year or longer. Many chutneys are made fresh daily but can be kept for a few days in the refrigerator. I sometimes freeze chutneys for later use. A little bit of chutney adds a lot of flavor.

MAKES 4
(1-CUP) SERVINGS

PER SERVING

Calories 100

Carbohydrate 14 g

Fat 0 g

Saturated fat 0 g

Dietary fiber 0 g

Protein 10 g

Cholesterol 5 mg

Sodium 150 mg

EXCHANGE

1 milk

PLAIN YOGURT
Dahi

Homemade yogurt is easy to prepare and tastes better than store-bought. Since I use a fair amount of yogurt, I prepare 4 to 6 cups at a time. It will keep in the refrigerator for up to 10 days. The secret is to refrigerate it as soon as it is set, otherwise, it becomes too sour. The homemade yogurt has more liquid whereas store-bought yogurt has gelatin or pectin to make it set more firmly. For culture, use only plain yogurt with active culture. Once you get the yogurt to set, use that yogurt for your culture. It will improve with age. Even if you don't plan to make yogurt on a regular basis, you can keep about 2 tablespoons of yogurt for culture in a airtight container for several days.

4 cups skim milk

¼ cup nonfat dry milk

2 teaspoons low-fat plain yogurt with active culture

Mix the skim milk and nonfat dry milk in a large saucepan. Bring to a full boil, stirring frequently to avoid burning at the bottom. (I usually boil the milk in the microwave for convenience; use a large enough bowl to avoid boiling over.) Cool the milk until lukewarm (about 110F, 40C). It should be warm to the touch. Add the yogurt to the milk and stir thoroughly.

Cover with a lid and keep in a warm place for 6 to 10 hours or overnight, until it is set. (I usually keep it in the oven, and in the winter I turn the oven light on to keep it warm.) Refrigerate for 2 hours or longer and serve cold.

MAKES 6
(½-CUP) SERVINGS

PER SERVING
Calories 50
Carbohydrate 7 g
Fat 0 g
Saturated fat 0 g
Dietary fiber 0.5 g
Protein 5 g
Cholesterol 1 mg
Sodium 237 mg

EXCHANGES
½ milk
1 vegetable

YOGURT WITH CUCUMBER
Kheere ka Raita

To make a nice accompaniment to any meal, serve this cool and refreshing combination of yogurt and cucumber.

2 cups plain nonfat yogurt

1 ½ cups peeled and grated cucumber

½ teaspoon salt

½ teaspoon Roasted Cumin Powder (page 49)

¼ teaspoon cayenne pepper (optional)

Stir the yogurt with a wire wisk in a small serving bowl.

Gently squeeze the cucumber by hand to remove the excess liquid. Add to the yogurt with the salt and stir to combine.

Garnish with the roasted cumin powder and cayenne pepper (if using). Do not stir. Serve immediately or cover and refrigerate until ready to serve.

PER SERVING

Calories 40

Carbohydrate 6 g

Fat 0 g

Saturated fat 0 g

Dietary fiber 0.5 g

Protein 4 g

Cholesterol 1 mg

Sodium 245 mg

EXCHANGES

½ milk

1 vegetable

YOGURT WITH TOMATOES AND ONION

Tamatar Piaz ka Raita

Serve this as a salad or an accompaniment to any meal.

2 cups plain nonfat yogurt

1 cup ¼-inch tomato cubes

½ cup ¼-inch cucumber cubes

½ cup finely chopped onion

¾ teaspoon salt

½ teaspoon Roasted Cumin Powder (page 49)

¼ teaspoon cayenne pepper (optional)

Stir the yogurt with a wire whisk in a small serving bowl.

Add the tomatoes, cucumber, onion and salt; stir to combine.

Garnish with the roasted cumin powder and cayenne pepper (if using). Serve immediately or cover and refrigerate until ready to serve.

MAKES 6
(½-CUP) SERVINGS

PER SERVING
Calories 72
Carbohydrate 13 g
Fat 0 g
Saturated fat 0 g
Dietary fiber 0.4 g
Protein 5 g

EXCHANGES
½ milk
½ starch

YOGURT WITH POTATOES
Alu ka Raita

If you like potatoes, try this combination.

> 2 small potatoes, boiled
>
> 2 cups plain nonfat yogurt
>
> ¾ teaspoon salt
>
> ½ teaspoon Roasted Cumin Powder (page 49)
>
> ¼ teaspoon cayenne pepper (optional)

Peel the potatoes and cut into ½-inch pieces. Set aside.

In a bowl, mix the yogurt and salt with a wire wisk. Add the potato pieces and stir.

Garnish with roasted cumin powder and cayenne pepper (if using). Do not stir. Serve immediately or cover and refrigerate until ready to serve.

YOGURT WITH BANANA
Kele ka Raita

This makes a great side dish or a light dessert. My children eat it like banana pudding.

2 cups plain nonfat yogurt

3 tablespoons sugar

2 ripe bananas

Mix the yogurt and sugar with a wire whisk.

Peel and slice the bananas into ¼-inch circles. Add to the yogurt and stir gently.

Serve immediately or cover and refrigerate until ready to serve.

MAKES 6
(½-CUP) SERVINGS

PER SERVING

Calories 100

Carbohydrate 21 g

Fat 0 g

Saturated fat 0 g

Dietary fiber 0.6 g

Protein 5 g

Cholesterol 1 mg

Sodium 58 mg

EXCHANGES

½ milk

1 fruit

MAKES 6 SERVINGS

PER SERVING
Calories 17
Carbohydrate 4 g
Fat 0 g
Saturated fat 0 g
Dietary fiber 1 g
Protein 1 g
Cholesterol 0 mg
Sodium 182 mg

EXCHANGE
1 vegetable

ONION AND TOMATO SALAD

Piaz aur Tamatar ka Salad

This salad is easy to prepare and is a colorful addition to any meal. Marinating the onions in salt and lemon juice reduces the pungency and makes them sweet and tangy.

> 1 medium red onion, cut into ¼-inch wedges
>
> 3 tablespoons fresh lemon juice
>
> 1 teaspoon salt
>
> 2 medium tomatoes, sliced into ¼-inch wedges
>
> ½ teaspoon freshly ground black pepper

Combine the onion, lemon juice and ¾ teaspoon of the salt in a bowl. Cover and marinate for 20 minutes or longer, stirring occasionally. Drain and discard the juice.

Add the tomatoes and sprinkle with the remaining ¼ teaspoon salt and black pepper. Toss lightly to mix.

Serve immediately or cover and refrigerate until ready to serve.

TOMATO, CUCUMBER AND ONION SALAD

Cachumber

PER SERVING

Calories 20

Carbohydrate 4 g

Fat 0 g

Saturated fat 0 g

Dietary fiber 1.4 g

Protein 1 g

Cholesterol 0 mg

Sodium 182 mg

EXCHANGE

1 vegetable

This low-fat salad tastes great with any meal. It takes a little time to chop all the vegetables but it's well worth the effort.

2 cups finely chopped tomatoes

1 cup finely chopped cucumber

½ cup finely chopped onion

¼ cup chopped cilantro

½ teaspoon salt

1 tablespoon fresh lemon juice

½ teaspoon Roasted Cumin Powder (page 49)

In a serving bowl, mix the tomatoes, cucumber, onion, cilantro, salt and lemon juice. Toss gently. Sprinkle with the roasted cumin powder.

Serve immediately or cover and refrigerate until ready to serve.

MAKES 12
(½-CUP) SERVINGS

PER SERVING
Calories 115
Carbohydrate 16 g
Fat 3 g
Saturated fat 0 g
Dietary fiber 5 g
Protein 6 g
Cholesterol 0 mg
Sodium 150 mg

EXCHANGES
1 starch
1 lean meat

MIXED BEAN SALAD

Chana-Rajmah Salad

Canned beans are used for this easy bean salad recipe. It keeps in refrigerator for up to a week and is good for brown bag lunches.

1 (16-ounce) can chickpeas

1 (16-ounce) can black-eyed peas

1 (16-ounce) can red kidney beans

2 tablespoons olive oil

1 garlic clove, crushed

½ cup finely chopped green onions, including 1 inch of the green tops

3 tablespoons chopped cilantro

1 hot green chile, seeded and finely chopped

¼ teaspoon Roasted Cumin Powder (page 49)

⅛ teaspoon freshly ground black pepper

½ teaspoon salt

3 tablespoons fresh lemon juice

Drain the chickpeas, black-eyed peas and kidney beans in a colander. Rinse with cold water. Pat dry with paper towels. Set aside.

Combine the olive oil and garlic in a small bowl. Set aside.

Mix the green onions, cilantro, green chile, roasted cumin powder, black pepper, salt and lemon juice in a large salad bowl. Add the beans and oil with garlic. Toss thoroughly. Cover with plastic wrap and refrigerate for 2 hours or longer.

MAKES 4
(½-CUP) SERVINGS

PER SERVING

Calories 38

Carbohydrate 6 g

Fat 1 g

Saturated fat 0 g

Dietary fiber 2.4 g

Protein 1 g

Cholesterol 0 mg

Sodium 288 mg

EXCHANGE

1 vegetable

CABBAGE AND CARROT SALAD
Gobhi-Gajar Salad

Serve this salad as a side dish with any Indian or Western meal. It is cooked to just the right tenderness and is mildly spiced.

1 teaspoon vegetable oil

½ teaspoon brown mustard seeds

4 cups thinly sliced cabbage

1 cup peeled and grated carrots

Pinch of turmeric

½ teaspoon salt

¼ teaspoon black pepper

Heat the oil in a heavy skillet over high heat. Add the mustard seeds, cover with a lid to avoid splattering and cook until the seeds stop popping, for a few seconds. Add the cabbage and carrots and then the turmeric, salt and pepper. Stir to mix. Stir-fry until heated through, 3 to 4 minutes. Do not overcook; the cabbage should be just barely tender.

Transfer to a serving platter and serve immediately.

RADISH SALAD

Muli Lachha

MAKES 4
(½-CUP) SERVINGS

PER SERVING

Calories 6

Carbohydrate 1 g

Fat 0 g

Saturated fat 0 g

Dietary fiber 1 g

Protein 0 g

Cholesterol 0 mg

Sodium 138 mg

EXCHANGE

free vegetable

For radish lovers, this is a nice change from the ordinary. It is usually served in the winter in India, when fresh, tender, long white radishes are abundant.

2 cups grated daikon radish

¼ teaspoon salt

2 tablespoons fresh lemon juice

Squeeze the excess water from the grated radish between the palms of your hands.

In a salad bowl, mix the radish, salt and lemon juice. Toss thoroughly. Cover and marinate in the refrigerator for 20 to 30 minutes.

STIR-FRIED SALAD

Phul Gobhi Salad

MAKES 6
(¾-CUP) SERVINGS

PER SERVING

Calories 33

Carbohydrate 5 g

Fat 1 g

Saturated fat 0 g

Dietary fiber 1.9 g

Protein 1 g

Cholesterol 0 mg

Sodium 214 mg

EXCHANGE

1 vegetable

Serve this salad for a colorful and refreshing accompaniment to any Indian or Western meal.

2 teaspoons vegetable oil

½ medium cauliflower, cut into small florets

1 medium green bell pepper, sliced

1 medium red bell pepper, sliced

1 small zucchini, sliced into strips

4 carrots, sliced crosswise

¾ teaspoon salt

½ to 1 teaspoon black pepper

Heat the oil in a heavy skillet or a wok over high heat. Add all the vegetables, salt and pepper. Stir-fry until heated through, 5 to 7 minutes. The vegetables should be tender but intact; do not overcook.

Remove from the heat, transfer to a serving dish and serve immediately.

MAKES 8
(½-CUP) SERVINGS

PER SERVING

Calories 110

Carbohydrate 19 g

Fat 1.5 g

Saturated fat 0 g

Dietary fiber 6 g

Protein 5 g

Cholesterol 0 mg

Sodium 180 mg

EXCHANGES

1 starch

½ lean meat

MARINATED CHICKPEA SALAD
Kabuli Chana Salad

This light salad is great with a sandwich or pulao. Marinating gives chickpeas a real zip, and the carrots add a crunchy texture.

> 2 (16-ounce) cans chickpeas
>
> 4 carrots, diced
>
> ½ cup green onions, chopped
>
> ¼ teaspoon salt
>
> ½ teaspoon coarsely ground black pepper,
>
> 2 tablespoons fresh lemon juice
>
> 2 tablespoons chopped cilantro

Drain the chickpeas in a strainer and rinse with cold running water. Pat dry with paper towels. Place in a salad bowl.

Add the carrots and green onions; mix well. Sprinkle with the salt, black pepper, lemon juice and cilantro, tossing to mix well. Refrigerate for 1 hour or longer.

MANGO SALAD

Aam ka Laccha

MAKES 16
(2 CUPS) SERVINGS

PER 2 TABLESPOONS

Calories 12

Carbohydrate 3 g

Fat 0 g

Saturated fat 0 g

Dietary fiber 0.5 g

Protein 0 g

Cholesterol 0 mg

Sodium 67 mg

EXCHANGES

free

In season, the sweet and sour taste of an underripe mango when combined with salt and cayenne pepper adds an excellent taste to any meal. It is eaten more like a pickle, in a small quantity, rather than like a salad.

> **1 firm, underripe mango (¾ pound)**
>
> ⅛ to ¼ **teaspoon cayenne pepper**
>
> ½ **teaspoon salt**

Wash and peel the mango. Slice the mango flesh into 1-inch strips. Discard the seed.

Toss the mango with the cayenne pepper and salt in a bowl. Cover and marinate for 30 minutes or longer in the refrigerator.

Serve cold or refrigerate for up to 2 to 3 days.

MAKES ABOUT
1 CUP

PER TEASPOON

Calories 1

Carbohydrate 0

Fat 0 g

Saturated fat 0 g

Dietary fiber 0 g

Protein 0 g

Cholesterol 0 mg

Sodium 44 mg

EXCHANGES

free

CILANTRO CHUTNEY

Dhania Chutney

The bright green color and the hot and sour taste of this chutney adds a zip to any dish. It is the most popular chutney served with meals or snacks. It is eaten with just about anything—from a rice pilaf to samosas, dal and breads or chicken and rice. It keeps well in the refrigerator for up to two weeks, although the color might change to dark green. I often freeze the extra to retain its bright green color.

1 small (3½- to 4-ounce) bunch cilantro

¼ cup coarsely chopped onion

½ teaspoon cumin seeds

1 to 2 hot green chiles

1 teaspoon salt

3 tablespoons fresh lemon juice

Clean the cilantro of any discolored leaves and stems. Cut about 1 inch from the tips of the stems. Leave the rest of the stems intact. Cilantro is often full of sand so wash thoroughly in 2 or 3 changes of water.

Place the onion, cumin seeds, green chilies, salt, lemon juice and cilantro in a blender and grind to a smooth paste.

Serve immediately or cover and refrigerate until ready to serve.

MINT CHUTNEY

Pudina Chutney

MAKES ABOUT
½ CUP

PER TEASPOON

Calories 4

Carbohydrate 1

Fat 0 g

Saturated fat 0 g

Dietary fiber 0 g

Protein 0 g

Cholesterol 0 mg

Sodium 66 mg

EXCHANGE

free

The refreshing flavor of this sweet and sour chutney is a nice accompaniment to any meal. Try this with meat dishes like kebabs or chops.

> 2 cups lightly packed fresh mint leaves (about 1 ounce),
>   cleaned and washed
>
> ⅛ teaspoon cumin seeds
>
> 1 hot green chile, chopped
>
> ¾ teaspoon salt
>
> 2 tablespoons fresh lemon juice
>
> 2 tablespoons sugar

In a blender, combine all the ingredients and grind to a smooth paste.

Transfer to a serving dish, serve immediately or cover and refrigerate until ready to serve. The chutney can be kept in the refrigerator for 1 to 2 weeks. It may change color over time, but the taste is unaltered. It can be frozen for later use. Freezing also retains the color.

TAMARIND CHUTNEY
Imli Chutney

MAKES ABOUT
2¼ CUPS

PER TEASPOON
Calories 14
Carbohydrate 4 g
Fat 0 g
Saturated fat 0 g
Dietary fiber 0 g
Protein 0 g
Cholesterol 0 mg
Sodium 55 mg

EXCHANGE
free

Tamarind has a unique sweet and sour taste. This delicious chutney can be used as a condiment with several dishes. It is made in many different ways. I like to cook mine, because it gives it a smoother taste and makes it keep for a much longer time—2 to 3 months in the refrigerator. And it can also be frozen for later use.

½ (3½-ounce) pack dry tamarind

3 cups water

1½ teaspoons salt

¾ cup packed light brown sugar

½ teaspoon cayenne pepper

Remove any seeds from the tamarind. Combine the tamarind and 2 cups of the water in a medium saucepan, bring to a boil and cook for 2 to 3 minutes. Remove from the heat. Let soak for ½ to 1 hour.

Grind the soaked tamarind in a blender. Strain the pulp in a strainer. Pour the remaining 1 cup of water over the pulp gradually, stirring with a spoon or your fingers to help strain the tamarind pulp.

Return the tamarind pulp to the saucepan. Add the salt, brown sugar and cayenne pepper. Stir until the sugar is dissolved. Bring to a boil over medium heat, stirring occasionally. Reduce the heat and simmer for 15 to 20 minutes. The chutney will thicken as it cools.

Serve at room temperature or refrigerate in an airtight container.

MAKES ABOUT
2 CUPS

PER TABLESPOON

Calories 8

Carbohydrate 1 g

Fat 0 g

Saturated fat 0 g

Dietary fiber 0 g

Protein 0 g

Cholesterol 0 mg

Sodium 68 mg

EXCHANGE

free

TOMATO CHUTNEY
Tamatar Chutney

I often make tomato chutney during the summer when tomatoes are abundant and inex-pensive. I also freeze some for later use. Serve this chutney with any dal or meat dish.

    4 medium firm, ripe tomatoes (about 1½ pounds)

    1 teaspoon vegetable oil

    ¼ teaspoon mustard seeds

    ¼ teaspoon onion seeds (kalonji)

    1 teaspoon salt

    1 hot green chile, seeded and chopped (optional)

    1 teaspoon coriander powder

    2 tablespoons sugar

Wash, core and coarsely chop the tomatoes. Set aside.

In a medium saucepan, heat the oil over medium heat. Add the mustard seeds, cover with a lid to avoid splattering and cook until the seeds stop popping, a few seconds. Add the tomatoes, onion seeds, salt, green chile (if using) and coriander powder. Cover with a lid and simmer for 15 to 20 minutes, stirring occasionally.

Remove the lid and cook until the chutney is of the desired consistency, 10 to 15 minutes, stirring occasionally. Stir in the sugar.

Transfer to a serving dish or store in an airtight container. The chutney will keep in the refrigerator for 2 to 3 weeks. It can also be frozen for later use.

COCONUT CHUTNEY

Nariyal Chutney

MAKES ABOUT
1½ CUPS

PER TABLESPOON

Calories 15

Carbohydrate 2 g

Fat 0.7 g

Saturated fat 0.5 g

Dietary fiber 0.7 g

Protein 1 g

Cholesterol 0 mg

Sodium 48 mg

EXCHANGE

free

Coconut chutney is very popular in south India where coconuts are abundant. It tastes great with Steamed Rice Dumplings (Idli; page 100) and Steamed Rice and Bean Cakes (Dhokla; page 66).

¼ cup chana dal (page 105)

1 whole dried red chile (optional)

½ cup coarsely chopped fresh coconut

½ teaspoon salt

½ cup water

¼ cup plain nonfat yogurt

In a small frying pan, dry-roast the chana dal and red chile (if using) over medium heat until the dal turns reddish brown. Remove from the heat and cool.

Grind the dal, chopped coconut, salt and water in a blender to a smooth paste. Stir in the yogurt.

Transfer to a serving dish. Serve immediately or cover and refrigerate until ready to use. It can also be frozen for later use.

PEANUT CHUTNEY

Mungfali Chutney

PER TABLESPOON

Calories 42

Carbohydrate 1 g

Fat 3.5 g

Saturated fat 0.5 g

Dietary fiber 0.6 g

Protein 2 g

Cholesterol 0 mg

Sodium 108 mg

EXCHANGE

1 fat

From the state of Maharashtra comes this very popular chutney. It is an excellent alternative to peanut butter. Serve with fresh or leftover roti or toast.

½ cup unsalted dry-roasted peanuts

¼ teaspoon cumin seeds

½ teaspoon salt

¼ teaspoon cayenne pepper

In a blender (preferably the small jar), blend all the ingredients just until the peanuts are ground and bind slightly. Do not grind too long as it will turn into peanut butter.

Store in a airtight container.

DESSERTS

Indian sweets are very different from Western ones. The variety of sweets available is endless. Some of the basic categories of sweets are *barfi, halwa, laddu* and *kheer*. There are no equivalent Western names. Chocolate is not served as a dessert, but it is available as a candy.

I have included some simple and easy-to-make desserts in this book. Indian desserts are typically high in fat and calories; I have kept the fat down wherever possible. By limiting frequency and quantity of desserts, one can enjoy a variety without compromising health.

CREAM OF WHEAT HALWA
Sooji Halwa

Here is the most popular halwa throughout India. It is often the choice of sweets offered as prasad (communion) at prayer meetings or at the temples. I grew up eating it for occasional Sunday breakfasts. Use ghee or butter for the special flavor and taste.

> ½ cup cream of wheat
>
> 2 tablespoons ghee or unsalted butter
>
> 2 tablespoons slivered blanched almonds
>
> 2 cups water
>
> ½ cup sugar
>
> 1 tablespoon golden raisins
>
> 4 cardamom pods

In a heavy saucepan, combine the cream of wheat and ghee. Heat over medium-low heat, stirring constantly, until the cream of wheat turns golden brown, about 15 minutes. Add the almonds and cook for 1 minute.

Add the water, stir and bring to a boil. Stir in the sugar. Cover with a lid, leaving it ajar to allow the steam to escape. Reduce the heat and simmer until most of the water is absorbed, 10 to 15 minutes, stirring occasionally. (Stir carefully to avoid being burned, because the halwa tends to splatter.)

Stir in the raisins. Transfer to a serving dish. Remove the seeds from the cardamom pods and crush with a mortar and pestle. Garnish the halwa with the cardamom powder.

RICE PUDDING
Kheer

MAKES 8
(½-CUP) SERVINGS

PER SERVING

Calories 200

Carbohydrate 28 g

Fat 5.5 g

Saturated fat 3 g

Dietary fiber 0.4 g

Protein 9 g

Cholesterol 18 mg

Sodium 123 mg

EXCHANGES

1 milk

1 starch

1 fat

Kheer is often referred to as rice pudding and is probably the most popular pudding in India. It does not taste anything like the Western rice pudding. It has a delicate, mild flavor. Traditionally, it is made with whole milk and cream, but here is a lower fat version. You will not miss the fat in this recipe. Although it can be made with skim milk, for best results, use low-fat milk.

> ½ gallon low-fat milk
>
> ⅓ cup basmati rice, washed
>
> 4 cardamom pods
>
> ⅓ cup sugar
>
> 2 tablespoons slivered almonds
>
> 2 tablespoons golden raisins

In a large, heavy saucepan, heat the milk over medium heat, stirring frequently to prevent sticking at the bottom of the pan. Add the rice and bring to a boil. Reduce the heat and simmer for 1 to 1½ hours over low heat, stirring occasionally to make sure the pudding does not stick to the bottom of the pan. Simmer until the pudding has reduced by about half. Remove from the heat; the kheer will thicken as it cools.

Remove the cardamom seeds from the pods and crush finely with a mortar and pestle. Add the sugar, almonds, raisins and cardamom powder to the pudding. Stir to mix.

Transfer to a serving container and cover. Serve warm or refrigerate and serve chilled.

CARROT SWEETS
Gajar Halwa

PER SERVING

Calories 271

Carbohydrate 46 g

Fat 5 g

Saturated fat 2.5 g

Dietary fiber 3.4 g

Protein 12 g

Cholesterol 17 mg

Sodium 182 mg

EXCHANGES

2 starches

1 milk

1 fat

In India this is a very popular dessert, especially in the winter when fresh carrots are available. I still make it in the winter although carrots are available here all year. Traditionally, it is made with milk and cream and roasted in ghee and is often cooked for hours to get the creamy taste and texture. Here is my quick and lower fat version with all the taste and half the hassle.

> 2 pounds carrots, grated
>
> 2 cups skim milk
>
> 1 (12-ounce) can evaporated skim milk
>
> 1 (15-ounce) carton part-skim ricotta cheese
>
> 1 cup sugar
>
> 4 cardamom pods
>
> 2 tablespoons slivered almonds (optional)

Place the carrots and skim milk in a heavy skillet over medium heat. Bring to a boil; reduce the heat and simmer for 20 minutes, stirring occasionally to prevent burning on the bottom.

Add the evaporated skim milk and cook until most of the milk is evaporated.

In the meantime, in a separate nonstick frying pan, cook the ricotta cheese over medium heat until most of the liquid is evaporated, 8 to 10 minutes, stirring occasionally to prevent burning. Do not stir too much. The cheese should become slightly crumbly.

Add the ricotta cheese and sugar to the carrots and mix. Simmer until most of the liquid is evaporated. The halwa should be moist, not dry and crumbly. Remove from the heat.

Remove the seeds from the cardamom pods and crush them with a mortar and pestle. Add the crushed seeds to the halwa.

Transfer to a serving platter and garnish with the almonds, if desired. Serve warm or cold.

MANGO ICE CREAM

MAKES ½
GALLON
(16 SERVINGS)

PER ½ CUP

Calories 118

Carbohydrate 20 g

Fat 3 g

Saturated fat 2 g

Dietary fiber 0.4 g

Protein 3 g

Cholesterol 12 mg

Sodium 44 mg

EXCHANGES

1 starch

½ fat

This recipe is adapted for an ice cream maker. The evaporated milk gives it a rich and creamy taste without adding the fat of traditional ice cream. For convenience use canned mango pulp.

> 2 cups half-and-half
>
> 1 (12-ounce) can evaporated skim milk
>
> ½ cup skim milk
>
> 1 cup sugar
>
> ¾ cup mango pulp or 1 cup mango slices, pureed
>
> ½ teaspoon mango extract (optional)

Mix all the ingredients in an ice cream maker. Make ice cream according to the manufacturer's instructions.

Serve from the ice cream maker or transfer to another containter, freeze and serve later.

CASHEW SWEETS
Kaju Barfi

PER PIECE

Calories 62

Carbohydrate 10 g

Fat 2.5 g

Saturated fat 0.5 g

Dietary fiber 0.4 g

Protein 1 g

Cholesterol 0 mg

Sodium 1 mg

EXCHANGES

½ starch

½ fat

Cashew barfi is a delicacy. Served at special occasions, it just melts in your mouth. It is often covered with an edible silver foil, which gives it an elegant look. The silver foil does not alter the taste in any way.

1 cup raw cashews

1 cup sugar

½ cup water

3 to 4 edible silver foils (optional)

Using a coffee grinder, grind the cashews to a fine powder. (A blender may be used, but it does not grind nuts as finely.) Set aside.

In a large skillet, place the sugar and water. Bring to a boil over medium heat. Reduce the heat and simmer until the syrup reaches the soft ball stage, 8 to 10 minutes. (To test for the soft ball stage, pour about ½ teaspoon of hot syrup into a cup of cold water. If the syrup makes a ball shape that flattens when picked up with your fingers, the syrup is ready.) Or cook to 230 to 240F (112 to 115C) on a candy thermometer. Remove from the heat.

Add the cashew powder and mix well. Cool until warm but cool enough to touch, 5 to 10 minutes, mixing occasionally to prevent drying. The cashew mixture will thicken as it cools.

Mix the cashew mixture thoroughly and pour onto a clean countertop. It will have the consistency of a dough. Using a kneading motion, form it into a smooth flat ball.

Place the flattened ball into the center of a piece of buttered waxed paper. Put another piece of buttered waxed paper on top. Using a rolling pin, roll out the dough to about ¼ inch thick. Remove the top piece of waxed paper. (If you want to use silver foil, carefully place on the rolled out dough. The silver foil is very delicate and it will stick to the barfi immediately. Once placed it cannot be removed.) Cut into 1-inch diamond shapes. Remove the bottom piece of waxed paper and place the barfies in a single layer on a plate or tray.

Allow the barfies to air dry for 20 to 30 minutes before storing in an airtight container. The barfies can be served immediately, kept at room temperature for up to 2 weeks, refrigerated for a month or frozen for later use.

COCONUT SWEETS

Nariyal Barfi

Barfies are typically diamond-shaped sweets. Here is a lower fat version that can be whipped up in a jiffy.

1 (15-ounce) carton part-skim ricotta cheese

1 ½ cups nonfat instant dry milk powder

1 ¾ cups sugar

1 ½ cups unsweetened shredded dried coconut

Grease an 8-inch square pan. Set aside.

In a large, nonstick frying pan, heat the ricotta cheese over medium heat. Add the milk powder and stir to mix thoroughly. Cook until most of the liquid is evaporated, 12 to 15 minutes. Stir frequently to prevent sticking or burning on the bottom.

Stir in the sugar. The ricotta cheese mixture will become liquid again. Cook 5 minutes, stirring occasionally. Add the coconut and mix thoroughly. Cook until the mixture is quite thick, 3 to 5 minutes.

Pour the mixture into the greased pan and press the mixture with a spatula. Cut into 1-inch diamond shapes. The mixture sets as it cools. Cool completely before removing from the pan.

MAKES 12 SERVINGS

PER SERVING

Calories 185

Carbohydrate 26 g

Fat 6 g

Dietary fiber 0 g

Saturated fat 3.8 g

Protein 7 g

Cholesterol 24 mg

Sodium 108 mg

EXCHANGES

1 starch

1 milk

1 fat

INDIAN ICE CREAM
Kulfi

Very popular in the summer in north India, kulfi is the original version of the ice cream available in India. It is sold plain or with phaluda (thin plain noodles). I remember visiting my grandparents in the summer and every afternoon eating kulfi on a stick bought from a vender who would come by yelling "Thundi thundi kulfi." This kulfi recipe is quick and lower in fat than the original but with the same excellent flavor.

> 4 cups low-fat milk
>
> 2 (12-ounce) cans evaporated whole milk
>
> 1 cup sugar
>
> ¼ teaspoon rose water (optional)
>
> 2 tablespoons pistachios, crushed (optional)

Using a nonstick frying pan, bring the low-fat milk to a boil over medium-high heat, stirring occasionally. Reduce the heat, continue to stir occasionally and cook until the milk is reduced to 1¼ to 1½ cups, 15 to 20 minutes. Cool to room temperature. Stir to break up any large chunks.

In a bowl, combine the evaporated milk, thickened low-fat milk, sugar and rose water (if using). Stir to dissolve the sugar. Pour the milk mixture into kulfi containers or ice cube trays (makes 2 trays). Freeze until solid. I sometimes freeze the mixture in frozen ice pop molds (makes kulfi on a stick).

Transfer into ice cream bowls and garnish with crushed pistachios, if desired.

♪♪

NUTRITIONAL OVERVIEW OF INDIAN MEALS

Typical Indian meals use liberal amounts of vegetables and grains. Because about one third of Indians are vegetarians, vegetarian meals are predominant in India. Those who are nonvegetarians eat meat and eggs in moderation. Hindus typically avoid beef and Muslims avoid pork. Overall, the diet is high in complex carbohydrates and fiber.

Fat and Cholesterol in Indian meals

Of general concern in the Indian diet is the liberal use of oil and *ghee* (clarified butter) in cooking. The food is often roasted or sautéed in ample amounts of *ghee* or oil or deep-fat fried. Therefore, the total fat intake of such a meal may be high. *Ghee* is often used in cooking, which increases the saturated fat intake. In several dishes of south Indian origin, coconut is used, which is also high in saturated fat.

I have modified the traditional Indian recipes to reduce the fat content. In some recipes *ghee* or coconut is used, but only in small quantities. Whenever possible, a liquid vegetable oil is used. Use your favorite liquid oil for cooking. It is well known that fat adds flavor to food, but the amount of fat needed can be reduced without altering the traditional taste and flavor. If any one method were to be called the Indian way of cooking, it would be roasting in a pan using oil. This process is called *bhun-na*. The spices are roasted in oil to make a *masala* (spice mixture), and then the meat or vegetables are roasted with the *masala* to bring out the flavor of the spices and the other ingredients.

This roasting also gives the sauce, or curry, its unique taste. The same *bhuna* taste can achieved by altering the process slightly.

Fat is an acquired taste. I always tell my clients that by gradually cutting down on their fat intake, their palates adjust and actually enjoy the real taste of food. Low-fat meals or foods feel much better to our system and we feel lighter and more energetic. High-fat foods are heavy in the stomach and we feel lethargic after eating them. One example of an acquired taste is that most people used whole milk not too long ago and now many have switched to low-fat or skim milk. Those same people now find whole milk too rich and not as palatable as they once did.

It is especially easy to eat low-fat foods if they taste good. I have made an effort to preserve the traditional flavor and taste, using only the minimum amount of fat to bring out the flavor and taste. Low-fat cooking is a good way to cut down on fat intake without compromising taste. A few fried foods and desserts are included to serve on special occasions.

Moderation and variety are the keys to good health. I have served low-fat meals to my unsuspecting family and guests for years; by the way they seem to enjoy the food, I would say they do not miss a thing. You will find these dishes easy to fit into most meal plans.

Cholesterol and Fat

Limiting fat and cholesterol are important steps you can take toward better health. The American Heart Association, American Institute for Cancer Research and the American Diabetes Association recommend a meal plan low in fat and cholesterol for better health and disease prevention. High fat diets are linked to heart disease, certain types of cancer, diabetes mellitus and weight gain. By understanding where cholesterol and fat comes from in your diet, it is easier to follow the recommendations set forth.

High blood (serum) cholesterol is one of the major risk factors for coronary heart disease. If your cholesterol is high, you need to find out how high it is and learn what you can do to lower it. The preferred way to lower your cholesterol is to modify your lifestyle.

Easy Tips to Reduce Fat and Cholesterol Intake:

◎ Use more fruits and vegetables. Five servings of fruits and vegetables per day are recommended.

- Use more high-fiber foods, like whole grains, dried beans, peas and lentils.
- Choose some meatless meals each week by using beans or lentils for a complete meal.
- Use less oil in sautéing or roasting spices.
- Avoid deep-fried foods or limit how often you eat them.
- Use condiments and spices to add flavor to recipes.
- Choose skim milk or 1 percent milk and its products. Choose nonfat yogurt and buttermilk.
- Avoid whole milk, cream, sour cream and half-and-half. Substitute evaporated skim milk or nonfat yogurt where possible.
- Limit the quantity of meat, poultry and seafood to six ounces (cooked weight) per day.
- Choose poultry and fish more often than red meat.
- Remove the skin from chicken before cooking.
- Choose only lean meats and trim all visible fat before cooking. Look for meat that has little or no marbling of the fat. Choose meats that have three grams or less fat per ounce.
- Avoid high-fat meats like spareribs, frankfurters, sausage and regular cold cuts.
- Use two egg whites instead of one whole egg in recipes.
- Limit the use of *ghee* and butter.
- Limit the use of coconut, coconut milk and coconut oil.
- Choose liquid oils, such as safflower, sunflower, corn, soybean, olive or canola oil, for most of your cooking.
- Choose a margarine that contains twice as much polyunsaturated as saturated fat.
- Use salad dressings sparingly. Use low-fat or fat-free dressings whenever possible.
- Nuts and seeds contain unsaturated fats, but in general are very high in fat. Use sparingly.
- Monitor the size of your portions. You can occasionally eat some things high in fat if consumed in small portions.

- Also you can eat too much of the right food. (Excess calories can be stored only as fat in your body.)

- Keep your fat budget in mind. If you go over your fat budget on one day, balance it the next day.

- Be aware of hidden fats. Hidden fats are in desserts, pastries, dairy products, prepared dishes and fried foods.

- Read food labels. Food labels can give you information on total fat, cholesterol and saturated fat. (**Rule of thumb**: If something has three grams of fat and one hundred calories, it has approximately 30 percent fat).

- One secret to serving low-fat meals: Do not tell your family or guests you have used a low-fat recipe or cut down the fat in the dish until after they have eaten and enjoyed it.

EXCHANGES FOR MEAL PLANNING
Weight-Loss Diets

All the research indicates that excess weight is linked to many serious illnesses including heart disease, high blood pressure, diabetes and cancer. Yet, as the years go by, people are getting heavier. Over the years what is healthy and acceptable seems to have changed. This is the era of weight-conscious people. We always seem to be reminded of what we can do to lose weight. Genetics aside, what we eat and how we live contribute to where the numbers fall on the bathroom scale.

Eating low-fat foods can lead to long-term benefits. Eating lower fat foods on a regular basis with occasional higher fat foods adds variety and avoids deprivation.

The portion size is very important. People feel they can eat all they want as long as the food is fat free or low fat. This is very misleading. Remember, a person can eat all the right foods, but if he or she eats more than what the body needs, weight gain will occur. The body knows only one way to store an excess intake of food (calories) and that is as fat.

Contrary to popular belief, eating healthy doesn't have to be boring or time consuming. Nor does it take special foods. Health and taste are not mutually exclusive. With a little creativity and careful selection, healthy dining can be enjoyed by the whole family and can taste divine. Here are some tips to help you begin eating healthy for life.

Many weight loss programs use the exchange lists for meal planning. This allows the individuals more variety and flexibility to plan meals. The exchanges provided for each recipe in this book can be easily calculated for meal plans.

A Word About Diabetes

Research clearly demonstrates that blood-glucose control effectively delays the onset and slows the progression of the long-term complications of diabetes: retinopathy, nephropathy, neuropathy and others.

Nutrition therapy is integral to total diabetes care and management. Nutrition and meal planning principles are among the most challenging aspects of diabetes treatment. It is important to have an individualized meal plan for achieving and maintaining desired blood-glucose levels. A registered dietitian (R.D.) can individualize meal plans based on the present nutritional status, lifestyle and medications needed to control diabetes.

The management of diabetes requires balancing food, activity and medication (insulin and/or oral hypoglycemic agents), if needed. When one eats, the blood glucose (sugar) levels rise. The first step in diabetes meal planning is making healthy food choices as it can affect blood glucose control. People with diabetes do not need special foods. In fact, the diabetic meal plan is good for the whole family.

Basic Suggestions for Management of Diabetes:

- ◎ Eat meals and snacks at regular times every day.
- ◎ Avoid skipping meals. Skipping meals or snacks can cause large swings in blood glucose levels.
- ◎ Eat about the same amount of food at the same time each day.
- ◎ Eat a wide variety of foods every day.
- ◎ Choose foods high in fiber like fruits, vegetables, whole grains and beans. High fiber foods are filling and may lower blood glucose and blood fat levels.
- ◎ Eat less added fat, sugar and salt.
- ◎ If one needs to lose weight, reduce portion sizes.

⊚ Physical activity and exercise can help improve blood glucose control. Exercise can contribute to the overall health of persons with diabetes.

⊚ Self-monitoring blood glucose levels can provide important information toward blood glucose control. Consult a physician if needed.

Exchange List for Meal Planning

FOOD GROUPS, EXCHANGE LISTS	CARBOHYDRATES, g	PROTEIN, g	FAT, g	CALORIES
Starches	15	3	0–1	80
Fruits	15	0	0	60
Milk				
Skim	12	8	0–3	90
Low fat	12	8	5	120
Whole	12	8	8	150
Vegetables	5	2	0	25
Meat and meat substitutes				
Lean	0	7	0–3	35–55
Medium high	0	7	5	75
High fat	0	7	8	100
Fats	0	0	5	45

A meal pattern based on the exchange lists enables an individual to exchange or trade one food for another in the same group. This helps include a wide variety of foods in the daily meals without affecting blood sugar significantly and at the same time keeps the calories and nutrient values consistent.

Each recipe in this book has the exchanges listed. Every effort has been made to calculate the best fit within the calories, carbohydrates, protein and fat in the dish. Please remember that the nutrient values for each exchange list are averages and are not always the exact values for a specific food within the exchange list.

Constant Carbohydrate Diet

Some people find that simply counting carbohydrates provides a more flexible approach than the exchange lists for managing diabetes. This method basically monitors carbohydrate intake. The principle of the constant carbohydrate diet is that all carbohydrates have a similar affect on blood sugar. In this approach, the starches, fruits and milk can be interchanged because they have approximately fifteen grams of carbohydrates per exchange or serving. The meal plan provides a suggested pattern of intake such as forty-five grams of carbohydrate at breakfast, sixty grams at lunch, seventy-five grams for dinner and twenty grams for a snack. In this approach, insulin can be adjusted based on the carbohydrate intake of the meal. The carbohydrate content of each recipe is given. Indian meals are typically high in carbohydrates. They can be easily worked into a constant carbohydrate diet.

EXCHANGE LISTS

The following pages list foods for each of the exchange groups and their nutritional content, as well as free and combination foods. Free foods have less than 20 calories per serving. The combination foods are those that represent more than one exchange group. The exchange lists also include foods specific to Indian meals. Each food is listed with its serving size, which is usually measured after cooking.

Starches

One serving has 80 calories, 15 grams carbohydrate, 3 grams protein and less than 1 gram fat.

Bread, dinner roll	1 slice (1 oz.)
Bun, hamburger or hot dog, English muffin, bagel	½ (1 oz.)
Cereal flakes, unsweetened	¾ cup
Cereal, cooked	½ cup
Crackers, low fat	6 to 8 (1 oz.)
Flour, wheat, white, corn	3 tbsp.

Pasta, noodles	½ cup
Pita, naan	½ (1 oz.)
Rice, cooked	⅓ cup
Tortilla, phulka, roti, chapati (6–7 inch diameter)	1

Starchy Vegetables

Corn, green peas, cooked	½ cup
Corn on the cob, 6 inches long	1
Mixed vegetables with corn, peas or pasta	1 cup
Potatoes, cooked	½ cup
Sweet potatoes, yams, plantains	½ cup
Squash, pumpkin category	1 cup

Beans (Count as one starch and one lean meat exchange.)
Dried beans, peas, lentils or dal, cooked	½ cup

Fruits

One serving has 60 calories, 15 grams carbohydrate, 0 grams protein and 0 grams fat.

Apple, banana, pear	1 small (4 oz.)
Dates, prunes	3
Cantaloupe, honeydew	1 cup cubes
Grapefruit, large	½
Grapes	17 (3 oz.)
Mango, small	½ fruit or ½ cup
Orange, peach, nectarine, kiwi	1 medium
Papaya	1 cup cubes
Plums	2
Watermelon	1¼ cups cubes

Raisins	2 tbsp.
Canned fruits packed in its own juice or in extra light syrup: pineapple, pears, peaches, cherries, apricots, fruit cocktail	½ cup
Fruit juice	
Apple, grapefruit, orange, pineapple	½ cup
Prune, cranberry, grape juice	⅓ cup

Milk

One serving has 90 calories, 12 grams carbohydrate, 8 grams protein and 1 to 3 grams fat.

Fat-free milk, ½%, 1%	1 cup
Evaporated skim milk	½ cup
Nonfat, low fat buttermilk	1 cup
Nonfat dry milk powder	⅓ cup
Plain nonfat yogurt	1 cup
Light, sugar-free yogurt	1 cup
Low-fat milk, 2% (5 grams fat)	1 cup
Low-fat yogurt, plain (5 grams fat)	1 cup
Whole milk (8 grams fat)	1 cup

Vegetables

One serving has 25 calories, 5 grams carbohydrate, 2 grams protein and 0 grams fat.

Vegetables that contain small amounts of carbohydrates and calories are on this list. Starchy vegetables are included in the starch list. If you eat one or two servings of vegetables from this list at a meal, you do not have to count the calories or the carbohydrates, because they contain only small amounts of these nutrients. (Raw vegetables, when cooked, decrease in volume.)

One vegetable exchange is as follows:

½ cup of cooked vegetables or vegetable juice

1 cup of raw vegetables

Beans: green, wax, Italian, Indian

Broccoli

Cabbage

Carrots

Cauliflower

Cucumber

Eggplant

Gourds: bitter, bottle, ridge

Greens: mustard, collard, turnip, spinach

Mushrooms

Okra

Onions

Pea pods

Peppers, all varieties

Radishes

Salad greens: lettuce, romaine, escarole

Tomatoes

Tomato/vegetable juice

Zucchini

Meat and Meat Substitutes

Very lean, lean meat and substitutes

One serving has 35–55 calories, 0 grams carbohydrate, 7 grams protein and 0 to 3 grams fat.

Beef, lean, less than 10% fat such as sirloin, chuck, round, rib eye, flank steak, tenderloin, ground round	1 oz.
Pork, lean, less than 10% fat such as ham, Canadian bacon, tenderloin, center chops, leg roast	1 oz.
Chicken, turkey (no skin)	1 oz.
Fish, any fresh or frozen	1 oz.
Shellfish: clams, crab, lobster, scallops, shrimp	2 oz.
Pheasant, duck, goose (no skin)	1 oz.
Luncheon meats, 95% fat free	1 oz.
Cheese	
Low-fat cottage cheese	¼ cup
Low-fat cheese (less than 3 grams fat per oz.)	1 oz.
Beans (Count as one very lean meat and one starch exchange.)	
Dried beans, peas, lentils and dal, cooked	½ cup

Medium and High Fat Meat and Substitutes

One serving has 75 to 100 calories and 5 to 8 grams fat.

Beef, most beef products fall in this category (5 grams fat)	1 oz.
Pork (5 to 8 grams fat)	1 oz.
Lamb: rib, roast, ground (5 grams fat)	1 oz.
Poultry: ground turkey or chicken with skin (5 grams fat)	1 oz.
Cheese	
Low-fat cheese (5 grams fat)	1 oz.
Regular cheese, American, cheddar (8–9 grams fat)	1 oz.
Paneer, whole milk (8 grams fat)	¼ cup

Egg (5 grams fat)	1
Tofu (5 grams fat)	½ cup
Processed meats such as regular luncheon meats, hot dogs, sausages, brats (8 to 9 grams fat)	1 oz.
Peanut butter (8 grams fat)	2 tbsp.

Fats

One serving has 45 calories, 0 grams carbohydrate, 0 grams protein and 5 grams fat.

Margarine	1 tsp.
Oil, vegetable	1 tsp.
Salad dressing	
Regular	1 tbsp.
Reduced fat	2 tbsp.
Nuts	
Almonds, cashews, mixed	6 nuts
Peanuts	10 nuts
Pecans, walnuts	2 whole
Seeds: sesame, pumpkin, sunflower	1 tbsp.
Saturated Fats	
Butter	1 tsp.
Coconut, fresh, grated	3 tbsp.
Coconut, dried	1 tbsp.
Coconut milk	1 tbsp.
Coconut oil	1 tsp.
Cream cheese	1 tbsp.
Ghee	1 tsp.
Half-and-half	2 tbsp.

Sour cream	2 tbsp.
Whipping cream	1 tbsp.

Free Foods

One serving of free food has less than 20 calories or less than 5 grams of carbohydrate. Foods listed without a serving size can be used as desired. Foods listed with a serving size should be limited to three servings per day and spread throughout the day.

Bouillon, broth, consommé	
Carbonated or mineral water, club soda	
Coffee, tea	
Condiments such as horseradish, lemon juice, mustard, soy sauce, vinegar	
Sugar-free diet soft drinks	
Sugar-free drink mixes, tonic water	
Spices, herbs, seasonings all	
Sugar-free gelatin, gum	
Sugar substitutes, aspartame, saccharin, acesulfame K	
Ketchup, taco sauce	1 tbsp.
Cocoa powder, unsweetened	1 tbsp
Jam or jelly, low sugar or light	2 tsp.
Salsa	¼ cup
Sugar-free hard candy	1 candy

Combination Foods

FOOD	SERVING SIZE	EXCHANGE/SERVING
Barfi, milk or khoa	1½ to 2 inches	1 starch, 2 fat
Cake, brownie, unfrosted	2-inch square	1 starch, 1 fat

FOOD	SERVING SIZE	EXCHANGE/SERVING
Chips, any	10 to 15 (1 oz.)	1 starch, 2 fats
Cookies, 2 in. diameter	2	1 starch, 1 fat
French-fried potatoes	10 to 12 (2 oz.)	1 starch, 1 fat
Halwa	½ cup	2 starches, 2 fats
Ice cream		
Regular	½ cup	1 starch, 2 fats
Low-fat	½ cup	1 starch, 1 fat
Kheer		
Whole milk	½ cup	1 milk, 1 starch, 2 fats
Low-fat milk	½ cup	1 milk, 1 starch, 1 fat
Pizza, thin crust		
Cheese, vegetarian,	¼ of 10 inch	2 starches, 2 medium-fat meats, 1 fat
Meat topping	¼ of 10 inch	2 starches, 2 medium-fat meats, 2 fats
Pudding		
Made with low-fat, milk	½ cup	2 starches
sugar free	½ cup	1 starch
Samosa, potato	1 medium	1 starch, 1 fat
Soups		
Bean	1 cup	1 starch, 1 lean meat
Cream (made with water)	1 cup	1 starch, 1 fat
Tomato or vegetable	1 cup	1 starch

Modified Exchange Lists are used with permission of The American Dietetic Association.

Sample Meal Plans Using Food Exchanges

Here is a sample of how to distribute daily calorie intake to obtain adequate nutrition. Make sure to divide the total exchanges into three meals and a snack if needed. If you choose not to have a snack, distribute those exchanges equally at the other meals. The total exchanges are used to calculate the nutrient distribution. The exchanges (pages 231–238) provide great variety and balance in meal planning. The recommendations for a well-balanced diet are less than 30 percent fat, 50 to 70 percent carbohydrate and 10 to 20 percent protein. Be careful of serving sizes and avoid skipping meals.

THE 1200-CALORIE DIET

Fat: 33 g (25 percent), Carbohydrate: 170 g (55 percent), Protein: 62 g (20 percent)

EXCHANGE GROUPS	TOTAL	BREAKFAST	LUNCH	DINNER	SNACK
Starches	6	2	1	2	1
Fruits	3	1	1		1
Milk	2	1		1	
Vegetables	2–4		1–2	1–2	
Meats	4		2	2	
Fats	3	1	1	1	

THE 1500-CALORIE DIET

Fat: 40 g (25 percent), Carbohydrate: 215 g (55 percent) Protein: 80 g (20 percent)

EXCHANGE GROUPS	TOTAL	BREAKFAST	LUNCH	DINNER	SNACK
Starches	8	2	2	3	1
Fruits	4	1	2		1
Milk	2	1		1	
Vegetables	2–4		1–2	1–2	

EXCHANGE GROUPS	TOTAL	BREAKFAST	LUNCH	DINNER	SNACK
Meats	5		2	3	
Fats	4	1	1	2	

THE 1800-CALORIE DIET

Fat: 50 g (25 percent), Carbohydrate: 245 g (55 percent), Protein: 85 g (20 percent)

EXCHANGE GROUPS	TOTAL	BREAKFAST	LUNCH	DINNER	SNACK
Starches	10	2	2	4	2
Fruits	4	1	2		1
Milk	2	1		1	
Vegetables	2–4		1–2	1–2	
Meats	6		2	4	
Fats	5	1	2	2	

THE 2000-CALORIE DIET

Fat: 55 g (25 percent), Carbohydrate: 275 g (55 percent), Protein: 95 g (20 percent)

EXCHANGE GROUPS	TOTAL	BREAKFAST	LUNCH	DINNER	SNACK
Starches	12	3	3	4	2
Fruits	4	1	2		1
Milk	2	1		1	
Vegetables	2–4		1–2	1–2	
Meat	6		2	4	
Fats	6	2	2	2	

For lacto-vegetarian or lacto-ovo-vegetarian diets (see opposite page) these distributions should work well. If the meat and substitute exchanges are too high, they can be reduced to three to four meat exchanges per day and substituted with milk or starch exchanges, without compromising nutrition. Eat a variety of foods within each exchange. Beans, lentils and pulses combined with other exchanges like grains or milk provide an adequate amount and variety of protein.

VEGETARIAN DIET

Being a vegetarian was considered a fad not too long ago in the United States. As the health benefits of vegetarian diet are being recognized, it is becoming more acceptable. Health organizations like the American Heart Association recommend that individuals should consume no more than six ounces of meat per day; so more and more, people are looking for alternatives. Many are becoming vegetarians or substituting some vegetarian meals in their diets. In this country the variety in vegetarian meals is often limited.

Thirty to 40 percent of Indians are vegetarians. Even Indians who are not vegetarians do not eat meat every day. During auspicious and religious occasions, Hindus are not usually permitted to eat meat. Indians have been vegetarians for centuries, and the variety in vegetarian meals is unlimited.

Vegetarian Meals

Indian vegetarian meals are unique in their composition and taste. Spices and the methods of preparation enhance the flavor of the food. Indian vegetarian meals are not limited to salads and steamed vegetables. Because of the varied tropical climate of India, the assortment of vegetables available are bounteous. As the ethnic population in the United States grows, the variety of tropical vegetables and fruits available also increases. Many dried beans and grains are easily available in Indian or other ethnic stores. Those who are following a vegetarian diet or would like a vegetarian meal should occasionally try an Indian vegetarian meal for variety and pleasure.

Types of Vegetarian Diets

Vegan: A strict vegetarian diet that excludes all animal products including eggs, milk and milk products.

Lacto-vegetarian: A vegetarian diet that includes milk and milk products.

Lacto-ovo-vegetarian: A vegetarian diet that includes eggs, milk and milk products.

Most Indians are lacto-vegetarians. Milk, yogurt and buttermilk are used extensively in the meal preparation and menu planning. Eggs are becoming more acceptable in Indian vegetarian diets. In the United States, lacto-ovo-vegetarian diets are the most prevalent.

Nutritional Adequacy of Indian Vegetarian Meals

Indian vegetarian meals (lacto-vegetarian), if planned properly, provide most of the nutrients needed. Choose a wide variety of foods to get all the necessary nutrients. Select a variety among fruits, vegetables, dried beans and whole grains. Keep the following nutritional needs in mind to obtain a healthy vegetarian diet.

Protein: Protein is found in most plant foods. Indian meals use an abundant amount of dried beans, nuts, whole grains, vegetables and dairy products. Most of the time one or more of these food groups are included in any given meal. Vegetarians do not need to worry about combining foods as the old "complementary protein theory" advised. It was believed that protein from different vegetable sources must be combined in appropriate ways to obtain adequate high-quality protein, called complementary protein. The latest recommendations indicate that the body will make its own complete protein if a variety of foods and enough calories are eaten during the day.

Calcium: Milk, yogurt and buttermilk are rich in calcium. Other good sources are dark leafy greens (such as mustard greens), dried beans and jaggery.

Iron: Good plant sources of iron include dried beans, dark green leafy vegetables, dried fruits, jaggery and fortified breads and cereals. Include foods rich in vitamin C (fruits, juices or tomatoes) along with iron-containing foods to increase iron absorption.

Vitamin B_{12}: Vitamin B_{12} is found in all foods of animal origin including eggs and dairy products; therefore, this is not of concern in most Indian vegetarian diets.

A WORD ABOUT SODIUM

The words *sodium* and *salt* are often used interchangeably, but they are not the same. Table salt is made up of sodium and chloride. Salt is the primary source of sodium in Indian diets. Sodium is an essential mineral, involved in almost all body functions including water balance, transmission of nerve impulses and maintaining normal muscle contractions.

Sodium and salt are found naturally in foods such as milk, meats and certain vegetables. Sodium adds flavor to foods such as breads, vegetables and prepared foods. Salt helps keep some foods safe, such as pickles, *papads*, chutneys and cheese, by preserving them.

The sodium content of each recipe is provided. Moderate amounts of salt are used in preparing the dishes. Salt can be adjusted to taste and individual requirements. Those who are on low-sodium diets should reduce or eliminate the added salt.

MAIL-ORDER SOURCES

Most ingredients should be available in your local grocery stores. For some special ingredients look for Indian grocery stores. Most international, health, organic and cooperative food stores usually carry most of the spices and beans. The ingredients can also be ordered by mail from the following companies,

Foods of India
121 Lexington Avenue
New York, NY 10016
PHONE: 212-683-4419
FAX: 212-251-0946

Bazaar of India
1810 University Avenue
Berkeley, CA 94703
PHONE: 510-548-4110
FAX: 510-548-1115

Kamdar Plaza
2646 West Devon
Chicago, IL 60659
PHONE: 773-338-8100
FAX: 773-338-8114

Merchant of India
5175 Sinclair Road
Columbus, OH 43235
PHONE: 614-846-1444
FAX: 614-888-3895

Indian Groceries and Spices
10633 West North Avenue
Milwaukee, WI 53226
PHONE: 414-771-3535
FAX: 414-771-3517

Spices of India
2020 N. Macarthur Boulevard
Oklahoma City, OK 73127
PHONE AND FAX: 405-942-7813

The Souk, Inc.
1916 Pike Place Market
Seattle, WA 98101
PHONE: 206-441-1666
FAX: 206-956-9387

The World Wide Web is transforming how we shop. Browse the Web and order your Indian groceries. Some of the sites available are listed below.

http//:www.indiaplaza.com
http//:www.namate.com

INDEX

INDIAN INDEX

About the Author

Madhu Gadia was born in India but has lived in the United States for several years. She is a registered dietitian and a certified diabetes educator. In addition to working part-time as a clinical dietitian, she teaches the art of Indian cooking across the United States. She is a member of the International Association of Culinary Professionals and The American Dietetics Association. She lives with her family in Iowa.